Inspirations
for ASSEMBLIES &
SCHOOL WORSHIP

Published by Scholastic Ltd,
Villiers House,
Clarendon Avenue,
Leamington Spa,
Warwickshire CV32 5PR

Written by Sandra Palmer and
Elizabeth Breuilly (ICOREC)
Edited by Christine Lee
Sub-edited by Jo Saxelby
Series designed by Juanita
Puddifoot
Illustrated by Kim Lane
Cover design by Clare Brewer
Cover artwork by Kim Lane

Designed using Aldus Pagemaker
Processed by Pages Bureau,
Leamington Spa
Printed in Great Britain by
Ebenezer Baylis & Son, Worcester

**British Library Cataloguing in
Publication Data**
A catalogue record for this book is
available from the British Library.

ISBN 0-590-53513-7 2nd revised edition
(ISBN 0-590-53017-8 1st edition)

CONTENTS

Introduction

For most of the day the good primary school is a busy hive of activity. Children are writing, reading, investigating, creating, problem solving, learning through play and so on, sometimes independently, sometimes with another child or in small groups. However, it is important that time is set aside for the children to come together as a class or school, thus giving them the feeling of being part of a community rather than separate individuals. It is to these times of assembly, and to the opportunities they present in enhancing the children's learning, that this book is addressed.

The legal position

The law recognises the importance of these times but considers that simply assembling pupils to hear school news, watch a small play or hear a story, is not enough. It requires that there be a daily act of collective worship, which should 'be wholly or mainly of a broadly Christian character' (Education Reform Act 1988). Responsibility for ensuring this in county schools lies with the headteacher. The right of the withdrawal from such worship sessions by pupils (at their parents' request) is safeguarded by the 1988 Education Reform Act [S.9(1)(3)(a) Handbook for Agreed Syllabus Conferences, SACREs and Schools].

Under the 1988 Act, the size and composition of the group concerned may vary. A primary school in which the whole school meets once a week for an act of worship, but in which there are also daily acts of worship in the classroom, would be meeting the demands of the law. Neither the time of day nor the length of the act of worship is specified.

BACKGROUND

Interpreting the 1988 Education Reform Act

The key issue in interpreting the ERA is what constitutes an act of collective worship, appropriate to the school context, which is wholly or mainly of a broadly Christian character.

The choice of words by the legislators is significant. These are not specifically Christian acts of worship, but rather acts of worship that are Christian in character. The former wording would suggest worship which is directed to an explicitly Christian understanding of God as Trinity: Father, Son and Holy Spirit; in which one might expect the worship of Jesus Christ as God. However, this would contradict other aspects of the Act. The use of the word 'collective' rather than 'corporate' in the 1988 Act, as in the 1944 one, is deliberate. The Act defines the county school as a 'collection of pupils of different beliefs and attitudes rather than a body or corpus of believers united by a common faith' (*Handbook for Agreed Syllabus Conferences, SACREs and Schools* (1989) REC).

The Act acknowledges that not all the children in a school will be Christian and that they may have different concepts of God, and that therefore the worship of Christ is inappropriate. The Education Secretary, in clarifying the Act, said that 'worship' is clearly intended to be such that non-Christian children can take part (letter from Kenneth Clarke to Fred Naylor of Parental Alliance for Choice in Education, 'School backed in dispute over act of worship', *The Guardian*, July 29, 1991).

However, children of other faiths are not the only non-Christians in the school. What of the children who are atheist or agnostic in background and/ or conviction? There are many in our schools. Is there a place in an act of worship for them? In a narrow interpretation of the phrase, as an act of giving adoration to a higher being, perhaps not. This clearly raises the problem of children either feeling excluded or being encouraged to be hypocrites.

One resolution of this dilemma is to think of an assembly in two parts, in which the majority is non-worship, with a prayer or hymn tacked on at the beginning or end as the 'worship bit' to fulfil the law.

We offer an alternative approach that is more in the spirit of the Act and that will serve all the national curriculums of the United Kingdom. This approach is based on a broader understanding of an act of worship, seeing it more as 'sacred time', a time which is qualitatively different from the rest of the day, rather than for the specific adoration of God. This sacred time includes times of celebration, of making welcome, of being silent and reflecting, of thinking of the needs of others, of mourning, of showing regret, of expressing commitment, and of being challenged to think from new perspectives. These are all activities which come under the umbrella of worship in the Christian tradition. We believe that assemblies which involve communal celebration, reflection or the challenge to think differently (though not necessarily all at the same session!) could be described as acts of collective worship which are broadly Christian in character. The general guidelines to planning an act of worship and the examples given in this book are based on this understanding of school collective worship.

Both the Education Secretary and the guidelines for the Act have made it clear that the use of non-Christian materials would not deprive an act of worship of its Christian character. This book draws on materials from a wide variety of sources, but handles them in the way that they might readily be handled from a Christian pulpit. It does, however, use materials which are consistent with the values inherent in Christianity and differentiates between the beliefs of a faith community, be they a tribal group or a world faith, and generally held views.

Using this book

When you look through this book you will find a variety of assembly types. Some need very little preparation; others are based on classroom work. Some are designed for the intimacy of the classroom;

others are appropriate for larger groups or the whole school. We have indicated where we think an assembly is only suitable for infants or juniors, but many of them can be adapted for different age groups. You know how much the children can listen to and how long they can sit still. Objects, pictures and other items that are necessary to the assembly, are listed under the heading, 'What you need'. Items which are not absolutely necessary but would enhance the assembly are marked as optional.

The majority of assemblies in this book are linked to the programmes of study in history, geography, maths and science, and are arranged accordingly. English skills permeate the classroom-based activities and the follow-up activities. However, these assemblies are not another means of delivering the statutory curriculum but an opportunity to enrich it. We believe that worship activities should be qualitatively different ways of thinking about the subject matter the children are investigating. Their classwork will involve investigating, categorising and using knowledge. Their worship should involve reflecting on, celebrating and sharing, not only what they have learnt, but their reactions to it.

These assemblies could be used as part of the study of a topic in class, a way of ending the topic or, in many instances, particularly in the history section, a way of initiating a topic. They lend themselves particularly well to the sort of planning where the whole school looks simultaneously at the one topic. However, they are not dependent on the subject being studied in class, so could be linked by the leader to the work of one class or be used totally independently of statutory curriculum timetabling, with references being made in the introductory sections to remind the children when they have studied for example, a period of history or a science topic. In this way, the assembly can be used like a play or a documentary on television. If the assembly deals with issues or a period of history the children have studied in the past, or are currently thinking about, it has an added meaning. If not, it may be drawn on when the topic is studied later, and meanwhile be of value in its own right.

Planning an assembly

This book offers a focus for assemblies. Except in rare instances, you are not given the total assembly outline because the context in which it is used will differ. Moreover, there are many activities which are important to the development of the school as a community which also need to take place regularly in assembly time – an essential part of the act of worship without being the whole of it. These include:
• celebrating the birthdays of children, members of teaching and ancillary staff;
• school announcements;
• remembering the needs of specific people in the school, for example spending time thinking about a child who has

been in a road accident, or a member of staff whose parent has just died;
• rejoicing with children and staff at key events in their lives, such as a birth, passing the driving test or getting a new job;
• welcoming and saying farewell to both short-term visitors and long-term members of the school;
• giving commendation awards for effort or improvement;
• hearing the news from a class and seeing their work.

Sometimes such activities can be the basis of a whole assembly, for example, saying goodbye to a class going on to secondary school. At other times they may be integrated with one of the assemblies. In this case, we suggest you do such activities first, so that the

children leave the assembly with the theme in their minds and have the chance to think on it. Likewise, even if you choose not to follow up the assembly in any depth, in many cases it would be appropriate to have a short discussion about it afterwards – not to tell the children how they ought to have interpreted it, but so that they are given the chance to articulate a response.

Although what we give in this book does not constitute the whole assembly, we have used the word 'assembly' in places as a 'shorthand' term for the units in this book – the focus and act of worship.

At the end of each assembly, we have included a suggestion for a short prayer or reflection. The chapter on prayer has examples of prayers which could be incorporated into various assemblies, as well as a discussion on prayer in school worship, and some examples of assemblies based around individual prayers, in particular 'The Lord's Prayer'.

You may find it useful to keep a record of school worship in order to ensure a balanced approach, and as a record for the school governors.

Surroundings

If assembly time is to feel different from other times of the day, the surroundings are also important. In most traditions an attempt is usually made to make the place of worship as beautiful as possible, whether in stark simplicity or by ornate finery, both to show honour to God and because of the simple, psychological truth that the physical surroundings affect the act.

The 1988 Education Reform Act specifies that the act of worship should take place on school premises. In the majority of cases this is the school hall, an area which is often also used for gym, dance, school dinners and fund-raising sales; the paraphernalia and equipment of which frequently invade the space. A school hall can, however, be transformed simply, in the way that a church hall may similarly serve a double function. A small table covered with a cloth and set with candles, flowers or an interesting artefact may make a difference, even if not directly referred to in the assembly. Similarly posters, scenes cut from calendars, or copies of paintings on a movable screen may provide a focus for the children. This would be there for the children as a backdrop for the week, perhaps commented on at the beginning or the end, but its primary function would be to create an atmosphere – as carvings, paintings and stained-glass windows do in a church.

The seating arrangement is another factor contributing to the atmosphere. Often space restricts the way the children

can sit, but a circle or semi-circle is conducive to creating a sense of community and an atmosphere of worship.

Another method of giving status to the act of worship and making it a focal point for the school is to have an assembly noticeboard. This can have on it items such as who is taking the assembly, the theme, details of the music and school news for the week. Follow-up classwork could also be put up on the noticeboard.

Music

Music also has a vital role in worship in the Christian faith. In the school context, it can be used while the children enter and leave the assembly, to listen to while they settle, and to listen to while they pause to think about what has been

said. Familiar music can give a sense of security, while new music from many traditions can add interest. The Christian faith encompasses a wide variety of music from choral singing to African masses. Suggestions have been made in the text where appropriate, bearing in mind that different schools will have different resources.

Communal singing has a well-established place in assemblies. We have suggested a number of songs and hymns, nearly all from the BBC *Complete Come and Praise* book, since this is commonly used in schools. Some of these hymns do contain specifically Christian references. However,

we do not think that the singing of a song necessarily implies a faith commitment on the part of the singer (plaintive love-songs are often sung by those content in a relationship) and, therefore, one is not imposing belief on the children. Moreover, a hymn often expresses a sentiment, such as joy in creation, which can be shared even if the theism is not. Schools will sing different bodies of hymns and religious songs, and have access to different collections, so ours are clearly only suggestions.

Stories in worship

There are a lot of stories in this volume and a number of story books are recommended.

It is worth looking closely at stories in the Christian tradition. Christianity is a story-telling faith. There are the stories about the life of Jesus and the Old Testament leaders and there are the parables of Jesus. His parables are not moral lessons in the way that Aesop's fables are. In such fables the moral is very explicit, which is why it can often be written at the end of the tale. The points of Jesus's

stories were not always clear, so often they left his disciples puzzled and bemused. Jesus told stories to illustrate an idea (such as the nature of God's love in the 'Prodigal Son') and to provoke his followers into thinking ('Who is my neighbour?' in the 'Good Samaritan'). He did not spell out the meaning for his disciples; he left them to figure that out and debate it amongst themselves. Futhermore the stories he told, and subsequently the story of his own life, often inspired people, giving them vision, a sense of purpose and of hope.

Jesus's use of stories seems appropriate for school worship for two reasons in particular. Firstly, it is educationally valid in that it does not impose

meaning on the child but encourages a personal response, within the framework of a common set of values: respect for self, others and the environment. Secondly, we are dealing with worship which is Christian in character and therefore the approach of the founder of Christianity is relevant.

There is a place for stories from many traditions which inspire, challenge and provoke the children into thinking about the questions of value and belief. However, we have avoided trying to draw any specific morals from the stories.

Conclusion

Christian worship is extremely diverse in its music, format and atmosphere. We hope that this book will help you plan diverse, thought-provoking, perhaps even inspirational, school worship for the children in your charge.

CHAPTER 1

Prayer

Prayer forms an important part of the Christian experience and almost invariably a part of Christian worship. This chapter includes:

• A discussion of prayer in the Christian tradition, and suggestions about the forms of prayer appropriate to the school context which are used throughout this book;

• Examples of worship focused on prayer in general or on particular prayers. The bulk of this section focuses on the 'Lord's Prayer' because it is universally used, but often poorly understood, by Christians.

This is intended to serve as an example of the way in which a particular prayer can form the focus of an assembly;

• Some prayers which you may want to use time and time again and are therefore not linked to one assembly.

Prayer in the Christian faith

In the Christian tradition prayer can take many forms. There are the formal prayers which have been said or sung repeatedly over the centuries. At times the words may be deeply felt or, because of the familiarity, may be simply a channel for approaching God. There are intercessions prepared by members of the congregation in their own words, with which others join in silently if they agree with the sentiment. There is the spontaneous prayer of the extemporary prayer meeting or of the individual alone. There is the simple lighting of a candle to remember someone before God, where all that might be said is a person's name. There is silence, as in Quaker meetings, where no words are uttered out loud, or maybe no words are framed even in the mind, because some things are beyond words. Icon painting in the Orthodox tradition shows how the act of creativity may be a form of prayer. This is even more obvious in the poems of John Donne and Gerard Manley Hopkins, and also applies to music-making. The overwhelming sense of joy and gratefulness in a beautiful view or a sleeping child is a form of prayer, as is the tear shed in joy, regret, sorrow or indignation.

As the forms for prayer vary, so do the reasons for prayer: being thankful, trying to bargain with God, expressing repentance, venting anger towards God, pleading for guidance, searching for reassurance or comfort, praise or petitions. Prayer may be chatting over the day's news, or it may be struggling with faith. What and how a person prays has as much to do with the individual's needs and personality as with his faith. What binds all these aspects together is that prayer, at its most basic, is the soul's feelings and longings, sometimes articulated in words, sometimes not, communing with the divine. For most Christians, the divine is named as the almighty Father God, for many the

Thank You for our Homes

divine object of prayer is Jesus the Son, and for some, prayer is addressed to the Spirit of God who is within all but who transcends all.

In the school situation there will be some, pupil and teacher alike, who will name the divine with the traditional Christian nomenclature. Many people of other faiths will be happy to speak to God as Father or Spirit, but not as the Son. Others may have no sense of the divine in traditional Christian terms, but may share some of the emotions and desires which are expressed in prayer, and may value the time of silence which can become prayer without words.

In view of this diversity of faith, which is often found in church schools as well as county schools, prayers in the name of Christ or addressed to Jesus are usually inappropriate for the school situation. They can result in embarrassment or hypocrisy or both. The central

prayer of the Christian faith, the 'Lord's Prayer', makes no mention of the name 'Christ'. We suggest that children be invited, rather than told, to join in with the words of a prayer or say 'Amen' to something they have heard. Thus it is clear that praying is an act of freedom, not something which should be imposed on anyone.

We also advocate the plentiful use of open prayer such as times of silence, reflection on a theme, expression of emotion in clapping, cheering and the like, and the use of the creative arts as a means of prayer. Of course, for some children the painting of a picture will be seen as nothing more than a craft activity or the chance for a chat with a friend. For others

it may be a time of reflection. However, all prayer in school, including formal prayer, is an offering of an opportunity. What is made of the opportunity is up to the child.

Infant children who have experience of prayer and who are encouraged to question and talk about all aspects of their experience will often ask pertinent questions and make thoughtful observations. However, the group reflection on an abstract issue which is initiated by an adult will be more ably handled by junior school children. Therefore such assemblies are all geared to that group.

1. What makes someone good at praying?

Assembly type
Junior assembly for class or larger group, preceded by classroom activity.

Stage 1 – Preparation

What you need
Paper, pens.

What to do
This assembly would fit well with a project to produce a mock newspaper. Although the final focus is on prayer, the preparatory stages should help the children to think about the personal qualities associated with vocations.

With the whole group, brainstorm a list of occupations (such as footballer, swimmer, teacher, school crossing person, hairdresser, doctor and so on). Ask the children to work in pairs to choose one vocation and write a job advertisement for it, conveying the qualities and skills needed to do the job. Ask each pair to compare their draft with that of another pair working on the same job.

Choose two children to rehearse and act out a scene showing two people reading through the job advertisements section of a newspaper over breakfast. Choose a third child to announce the scene.

Stage 2 – Assembly

What you need
The job advertisements (see Preparation) pasted inside a mock or real newspaper, props for a breakfast scene.

What to do
Let the children introduce and then act out their play, pretending to be looking for a job and reading out the job advertisements. (Alternatively, if none of the children are sufficiently confident about this, read them out yourself, making appropriate comments.)

After the performance, point out to the children that different jobs require different skills and experience. Emphasise that people are good at different things. Then pose this question: 'What makes someone good at praying?' This is a difficult question and it may remain rhetorical, especially in a whole school assembly, but you might make suggestions, 'Perhaps it is...'.

Then read this excerpt from Samuel Taylor Coleridge's *The Rime of the Ancient Mariner*.

He prayeth well, who loveth well
Both man and bird and beast,
He prayeth best, who loveth best
All things both great and small;
For the dear God loveth us,
He made and loveth all.

Prayer/reflection
Ask the children to listen to the words from the poem again and to consider how Coleridge answered the question of who was good at praying.

Song/hymn
It is possible to sing a version of Coleridge's words as a hymn by adding the following two lines after the first two quoted above:
And he that loveth all God made
That man he prayeth best.
The lines then fit any 8.6.8.6. tune.
Come and Praise
73 When your Father made the world
74 Sad, puzzled eyes
79 From the tiny ant

2. Prayer of St Francis

Assembly type
School assembly for juniors based on a classroom drama activity.

Stage 1 – Preparation

What you need
A copy of the prayer of St Francis, a picture of St Francis (optional).

What to do

Lord make me an instrument of your peace.

Where there is hatred, let me sow love;

Where there is injury, pardon;

Where there is discord, union;

Where there is doubt, joy...

These words are the opening lines of what has come to be known as the prayer of St Francis, although they were written in the nineteenth century. They do, however, stand in the tradition of St Francis's life of humility and service.

Read the whole prayer with the class, then divide them into small groups to work on one line each. Ask them to discuss the meaning of the words and then to make up a very short play illustrating the meaning of the words. Ask the children to re-enact their plays in front of the rest of the class.

Stage 2 – Assembly

What you need

An overhead projector (optional).

What to do

Before the assembly, write out the prayer on an overhead projector transparency or poster.

Introduce the assembly by reading out the words, inviting the children to join in and explaining that you've been thinking about them in your class. Then ask the children to act out their plays for each line.

Prayer/reflection

Invite the children to say the words with you.

Song/hymn

Come and Praise
147 Make me a channel of your peace

The Lord's Prayer

The Lord's Prayer is almost universally said or sung as part of worship by Christians throughout the world. The gospels say that this was the prayer that Jesus taught his disciples and it has been used ever since. It has often been gabbled, apparently meaninglessly, by children in school and church and for this reason some teachers have understandably been reluctant to use it. The counterview is that learning the prayer by rote gives children access to it later, at a time when they might need it. When people are in need of reassurance or of something ritualistic to say, many reach for the Lord's Prayer to give them calm. Saying it can also give the children the sense of belonging to a greater and older community than the one of which they are immediately aware.

The purpose of this series of activities and assemblies is to bridge the two positions. The Lord's Prayer is a difficult

prayer for adults as well as children, rooted as it is in the historical situation of first century Palestine. Nevertheless, some insight can be gained by children whose horizons are broadening and who are beginning to gain concepts of other times, places and languages.

We have chosen to stick to the traditional version found in the King James Bible (Authorised Version), as this is the most familiar, and modernising the translation doesn't make it much easier to comprehend, unlike other parts of the Bible. You could, however, use any version with which you feel comfortable. A musical setting is given in *Come and Praise*. This could be used for the first and last assemblies in the series, and for some of the others.

The Lord's Prayer is a prayer which should be theologically acceptable to both Jews and Muslims as well as Christians. It is the association with Christianity which might make a non-Christian reluctant to join in, rather than its essential meaning.

1. Introducing the Lord's Prayer

Assembly type
Junior class or larger group, teacher-led assembly.

What you need
The Lord's Prayer on a poster or overhead transparency, copies of photocopiable pages 124 and 125.

What to do
Show the children the words of the Lord's Prayer and read it to them. Ask them if they know what it is and where they may have heard it before. Distribute copies of photocopiable page 124, and explain to the children that you would like them to try to join in with the opening lines of the Lord's Prayer in the various languages

shown.

Adapt the assembly text on page 125 to your own style.

Prayer/reflection
Invite the children to join with you to say the Lord's Prayer as a prayer or simply to listen to the words.

Song/hymn
Sing a musical setting of the Lord's Prayer, such as *Come and Praise* 51.

Further activity
Enlist the help of children and parents to build up a display of the opening words of the Lord's Prayer in as many different languages as possible.

Dear Mr Kewley My friend Matthew is always happy. He always plays with me at play time

2. Our Father

Assembly type
Junior class or larger group assembly, preceded by classroom activity.

Stage 1 – Preparation

What you need
Copies of photocopiable page 126, paper, pens, coloured pens.

What to do
Distribute copies of photocopiable page 126, and ask the children to think about the poster. Do they know anyone who fits one of the characteristics or even all of them?

Ask them to write letters to you naming and describing the people concerned and to draw their faces on the posters. You may find they write about their fathers, mothers, friends, siblings or even teachers. Choose some to read out loud, but remember to ask the children's permission to use them.

Stage 2 – Assembly

What you need
The selected letters in reply to the poster, copies of the poster, display materials, the words of the Lord's Prayer written out on a poster or overhead transparency, a Bible, copy of photocopiable page 127.

What to do
Before the assembly, make a display of the posters and the letters. Talk about the poster and read out some of the replies, pointing out that the children have connected specific people with the characteristics mentioned.

Draw attention to any that mention a father. Show the children a Bible and draw their attention to the gospels, reminding them that these contain the words that the early Christians wrote down about Jesus.

Adapt the assembly text on page 127 to your own style. If the children are familiar with the word 'metaphor', use it.

Prayer/reflection
Remind the children of their replies to the poster and how a number of different people fitted the description, not just fathers.

For each person who comforts us

For each person who encourages us

For each person who helps us

For each person who takes away our fears

We are thankful.

Song/hymn
Come and Praise
54 The King of love and 56 The Lord's my shepherd (both are settings of Psalm 23)
62 Heavenly Father

3. Who art in heaven

Assembly type
Junior class or whole school assembly.

What you need
A cassette player; some lively, happy music (such as the music representing the dancing snowmen from *The Snowman* by Howard Blake) and some peaceful music (such as the first movement of Beethoven's 'Pastoral' Symphony (No 6), sitar music or a harp concerto); pictures of peaceful gardens, cartoons of angels playing harps, a painting of God in the clouds (such as Blake's *The Ancient of Days*) (optional), the Lord's Prayer written out on an overhead projector transparency, copy of photocopiable page 128.

What to do
While one objective of this assembly is that the children gain insight into the Lord's Prayer, another is that they become aware of the diversity of views with regard both to heaven and to interpretations of Jesus's sayings. Furthermore, it is hoped that the children will begin to consider different ideas about heaven, rather than holding on to fixed ones, as some may do. Before the assembly, prepare a display illustrating different concepts of heaven. Include pictures of gardens, cartoons about heaven and paintings about God.

Remind the children of the previous assembly on 'Our Father', and explain that today you'll be considering the words, 'Who art in heaven'. Tell them that in modern English, it is simply 'Our Father in heaven'.

Then adapt the assembly text on page 128 to your own style.

Prayer/reflection
Play some lively, happy music and ask the children to think about heaven as a happy place where people have fun. Then play some peaceful music and ask the children to imagine a peaceful heaven. Invite the children to come and look at the display later in the day, perhaps at playtime.

Song/hymn
Come and Praise
140 The peace prayer (Lead me from death to life)
141 Shalom
144 Peace is flowing
149 The vine and the fig tree (And ev'ryone beneath the vine)

Further activities
• Ask the children to paint a picture of one of the images of heaven presented in the assembly, or one that they imagine themselves. Display the pictures with a caption such as 'Our pictures of heaven. If it exists what do you hope it will be like?' Some children, especially Muslims, may feel it is wrong to paint a representational picture of heaven. Encourage them to produce an abstract picture, perhaps with beautiful patterns.
• Ask the children to discuss first, and then make up a travel advertisement extolling the virtues of their heaven. They might use a desktop publishing program on the computer for this.

4. Hallowed be thy name

Assembly type
Junior class or larger group assembly.

What you need
The Lord's Prayer on a poster or overhead transparency; a copy of *Please, Mrs Butler* by Allan Ahlberg, copy of photocopiable page 129.

What to do
Remind the children of the first assemblies about the Lord's Prayer and then explain to them that you are going to think about what 'Hallowed be thy name' means, especially since so many children praying over the centuries have misheard the words and thought God's name was Harold.

Then ask the children to think about whether they have ever done something wrong, and have used as an excuse, 'But he told me to do it, miss'. Read to them the poem 'Blame' found in Allan Ahlberg's anthology, *Please, Mrs Butler*.

Adapt the assembly text on page 129 to your own style.

Prayer/reflection
Invite the children to repeat after you:

May God's name be kept out of wicked acts.
May God's name be kept holy.
May God's name be hallowed.

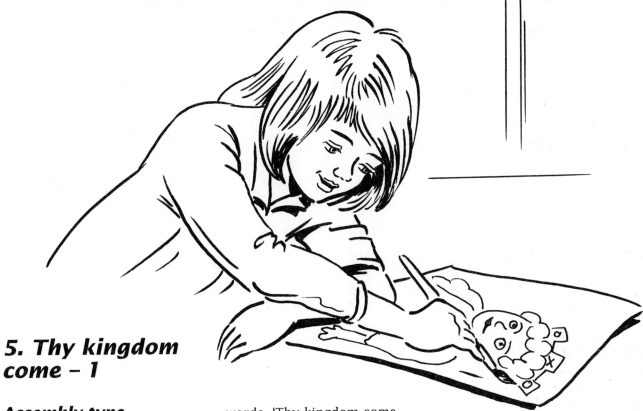

5. Thy kingdom come – 1

Assembly type
Junior class or larger group assembly preceded by classroom activity.

Stage 1 – Preparation

What you need
The words of the Lord's Prayer, information books on current affairs and history, pictures of world leaders past and present (such as kings, queens, presidents, prime ministers and dictators), chalkboard, cuttings about rulers from newspapers, pens, paper, paints.

What to do
Remind the children that the current series of assemblies is about the Lord's Prayer, and tell them that you need their help in preparing and presenting it. Discuss the words, 'Thy kingdom come, thy will be done on earth as it is in heaven' and draw their attention to the key word of 'kingdom'. Tell them that today you are considering earthly kings and rulers and ask them to name some, living or dead. Show them the collection of pictures and ask if they can recognise any of the people shown.

Make a list of rulers and royalty on the board, including some elected by a democratic process. Identify with the children some key questions for research.
• How did they become the ruler?
• How much power did they have?
• How did other people regard them and why? Were they considered to be good or bad, powerful or ineffectual or is it too early to tell?

Ask the children to work in threes, with two writing a profile of their ruler or royal person, and the third painting his or her portrait.

Stage 2 – Assembly

What you need
The portraits or pictures of the rulers and royalty on display, the prepared profiles of the different rulers and royalty, a poster or overhead transparency of the Lord's Prayer, copy of photocopiable page 130.

What to do
Remind the children that you are looking at the Lord's Prayer. Read the relevant lines and tell them that today you are looking at the idea of God's

kingdom, but you are going to start by thinking about earthly kings and rulers. Ask some of the children to read their profiles.

Adapt the assembly text on page 130 to your own style.

Prayer/reflection

Invite the children to listen to the words from the Anglican Alternative Service Book (1980) about those in authority:

Bless and guide Elizabeth our Queen; give wisdom to all in authority; and direct this and every nation in the ways of justice and of peace; that [people] may honour one another, and seek the common good.
(adapted from the 'Intercessions' in the Order for Holy Communion, Rite A)

Song/hymn

Come and Praise
48 Father, hear the prayer we offer (Explain to the children that this would be a good hymn for a ruler to sing.)

6. Thy kingdom come – 2

Assembly type

Junior class or larger group assembly.

What you need

Poster or overhead transparency of the Lord's Prayer, a modern translation of the Bible, such as the Good News Bible (Today's English Version), or the Jerusalem Bible is particularly clear, copy of photocopiable page 131.

What to do

Before the assembly, prepare some of the children to read one each of the 'Beatitudes' from Matthew 5:2-10. They will need to stand in the order in which they are reading. The Beatitudes are not easy to understand. Indeed, scholars debate extensively about them, but they do convey Jesus's constant concern for the outcast. The children may grasp this, or may simply tune in to the rhythm of the words.

The assembly also highlights two issues on which there is divergence of views in Christianity:
• whether God's kingdom is in this life or the next;

• whether or not Jesus was abolishing the old law of Moses and replacing it with the law of loving God and one's neighbour, or whether he was stating the underlying principle of God's laws.

Remind the children about the previous assembly when they thought about the nature of God's kingdom. Then explain to them that they are going to hear what Jesus said about the people to whom the kingdom belonged.

Ask the readers to read the passage about the Beatitudes.

Tell the children that Jesus was saying that unlike most earthly rulers, God is concerned about the welfare of the poor and those that society has rejected.

Remind the children that all countries have rules and laws. What were God's laws according to Jesus? He said that all God's laws were summarised in two sentences: Love God with all your heart, soul and mind; and, love your neighbour as yourself (Matthew 22:37-40).

Adapt the assembly text on page 131 to your own style.

Prayer/reflection

Listen to the sentence again from the Lord's Prayer and think about what it means.

Song/hymn
Come and Praise
42 Travel on
58 At the name of Jesus
64 The wise may bring their learning
70 Cross over the road
75 Bread for the world
88 I was lying in the roadway
148 Let the world rejoice together

Further activities
• Find out more about one of the Christian charities who work for the poor, such as Christian Aid or Barnardos. This could be reported in another assembly.
• Discuss with the children whether they think people need more rules than simply loving your neighbour as yourself.
• Tell the story of the 'Good Samaritan' (Luke 10:25-37) and discuss it with the children, explaining to them that the Jews and Samaritans were enemies, so the Jew would have been surprised that a Samaritan helped him. Then ask the children to write the story in their own words or, if they want, to make up their own version. Let the children work in groups of about six to make a play from their story.

7. Daily bread

Assembly type
Junior class or larger group assembly.

What you need
The Lord's Prayer on a poster or overhead transparency, different types of bread, pictures of refugee children, copy of photocopiable page 132.

What to do
What Jesus actually meant by the word which has been translated as 'daily' is a matter of some discussion, as there is no direct equivalent in English. However, within the Christian tradition, the petition has commonly been interpreted as being about asking for the day's needs, and this is how we have interpreted it.

Ask for a show of hands of how many children had bread to eat yesterday, and remind them of all the times in the day when they might have done so (breakfast, sandwiches, afternoon tea). If readily available, show them different types of bread and see if they can name any of them. Explain to them that bread is eaten in many parts of the world as the food that 'fills you up'. Draw their attention to the fact that in some parts of the world, such as China, rice is eaten instead. Then continue, adapting the assembly text on page 132 to your own style.

Prayer/reflection
Ask the children to look at pictures of a refugee camp or a drought-stricken area and to think quietly of those who do not know whether they will have their daily bread.

Song/hymn
Come and Praise
77 Desert rain (The sun burns hot)
87 Give us hope, Lord
94 Mother Teresa's prayer (Make us worthy, Lord)
139 The sharing bread (Now the harvest is all gathered)

Further activities
• Using material from one of the aid charities (see Resources, page 192), initiate a project to find out more about problems of hunger, and the causes of it.
• Ask the children to make up their own grace for a staple food or some food they particularly like.

8. Forgive us our trespasses

Assembly type
Junior class or larger group assembly preceded by classroom activity.

Stage 1 – Preparation

What you need
Paper, pens.

What to do
Forgiveness is a central theme in Christianity. Sometimes, though, it can be presented too lightly. There are times when it may be important to be angry first and to allow the forgiveness to come with time and will. This is particularly important to remember when it comes to the issue of child abuse, as children can be all too forgiving of adults, to their own emotional and physical cost.

The language of the Lord's Prayer is difficult on this point and probably best recognised as such: modern translations such as 'sin' are no easier for the children to understand and may be even more confusing.

Talk to the children about the sort of things which make them feel hurt or angry, being aware of the fact that some of them might not want to make public statements. It is probably best to talk about things in the abstract rather than encouraging them to recall and narrate the pain of particular times. Share with them the sort of things that make you feel hurt or let down by someone. Ask the children to recall whether they have ever hurt anyone else or let them down, perhaps deliberately, perhaps without meaning to. Now ask the children to write something short about both issues, telling them that you would like to use the material in assembly, but stressing that you would ask their permission first and keep the material anonymous.

Stage 2 – Assembly

What you need
The Lord's Prayer on a poster or overhead transparency, a selection of the children's writing, some peaceful music, copy of photocopiable page 133.

What to do
Tell the children that you have been discussing being hurt and hurting others with one class and read out some of the things that the children have written.

Talk about how hard it can be sometimes to forgive people who hurt you, because the pain can go very deep. Sometimes you have a quarrel with someone and say, 'I am never going to talk to that person again.'

Adapt the assembly text on page 133 to your own style.

Prayer/reflection
Forgiving people is a way of making peace with them, so let us now listen to peaceful music.

Song/hymn
Come and Praise
68 Kum ba yah
91 Break out (You can build a wall)
140 The peace prayer (Lead me from death to life)
141 Shalom
147 The prayer of St Francis (Make me channel of your peace)
149 The vine and the fig tree (And ev'ryone beneath the vine)

9. The time of trial

Assembly type
Junior class or larger group assembly.

What you need
The Lord's Prayer on a poster or overhead transparency, copy of photocopiable page 134.

What to do
The last part of the Lord's Prayer is also quite difficult to understand. Most scholars see it as a plea for God's help to maintain faith through fearful times when it might be lost. In terms of Jesus's own life, the prayer is a parallel to his own plea in the garden of Gethsemane, that he would not have to face the agony ahead, but then that he would have the faith to continue if he had to go through with the Crucifixion (Luke 22:41-44). Modern translations are probably more in tune with the original meaning: 'Do not bring us to the time of trial'.

Children have their own fears which are analogous to

those of Jesus and his disciples – the fear of a nuclear war is a common one, as increasingly is anxiety about the earth's destruction through environmental damage. Deep fear about the death of parents is also very common at this age. However, it is probably best to talk about fears in general terms rather that naming them, to avoid adding to the children's anxieties.

The final sentences of the Lord's Prayer are not Biblical and were added by the early Church.

Read through the Lord's Prayer with the children. Tell them that scholars who study the Bible are not certain what this sentence means but many of them think it should read,

'Do not bring us to the time of trial.' Explain that you are going to try and help them understand what that means, then adapt the assembly text on page 134 to your own style.

Prayer/reflection
We've talked about fears, but we can also look forward to the future with hope so let's sing a hymn about something cheerful and full of hope.

Song/hymn
Come and Praise
19 He's got the whole world
31 God has promised
43 Give me oil in my lamp
44 He who would valiant be
45 The journey of life
89 Guess how I feel

10. Conclusion

Assembly type
Junior class or larger group assembly.

What you need
The words of the Lord's Prayer on a poster or overhead transparency, a string of beads, copy of photocopiable page 135.

What to do
The Lord's Prayer is both a public and private liturgical prayer. Some Christians have found it a spiritual resource while giving it little intellectual meaning. While one would hope that the children have gained some understanding of it through this series of assemblies, nevertheless it can also have this meditative, mystical function for them. This assembly focuses on that function.

Ask the children to sit very still and quiet and close their eyes and just listen, then adapt the assembly text on page 135 to your own style.

Song/hymn
Come and Praise
51 The Lord's Prayer

Further activity
Ask the children to write contributions from their own experience for a class book titled, 'How to get calm'.

Prayers to use for particular occasions

This is not meant to be an exhaustive list, but rather a variety of examples of how you can reflect on or celebrate events that are important to the children and staff, whether these are local to the school community or of wider importance.

Prayers at parting

The following are benedictions for departure and separation, whether this is simply overnight, or a longer parting. They are particularly appropriate when the act of worship is at the end of the day, whether in the hall or classroom. They are a way of wishing well to those departing and of expressing a desire for safe return. If you use them regularly, the children will gradually become familiar with them and join in.

The night falls and wraps our world in darkness.
In our going and in our returning
May we be kept safe.
Amen.

A variation on the Christian grace:
May the kindness of our friends,
The love of our family
And the fellowship of our community
Keep is all now and in time to come.
Amen.

May peace surround us,
Love enfold us
And compassion stir us,
Now and for always.
Amen.

Bless to me the moon above my head;
Bless to me, the earth on which I tread.
Bless to me my family, friends and all.
May I a blessing to them be
As they a blessing are to me.
Amen.

May we be blessed
In our sleep with rest,
In our dreams with vision,
In our waking with a calm mind,

In our souls with friendship.
(adapted from *A Wee Worship Book*, Wild Goose Worship Group) Used by Permission

From the Native American tradition:
Deep peace of the running wave to you
Deep peace of the flowing air to you
Deep peace of the quiet earth to you
Deep peace of the shining stars to you
Deep peace of the son of peace to you.

The Lord bless you and keep you;
The Lord make his face shine upon you and be gracious to you;
The Lord turn his face towards you and give you peace.
(Numbers 6:24-26, New International Version)

For the sick
Adapted from the Anglican Alternative Service Book, from the 'Intercessions' in the Order for Holy Communion, Rite A: Comfort and heal all those who suffer in body, mind, or spirit, especially (names); give them courage and hope in their troubles, and bring them joy and peace.

We think of all those who are ill,
All those who are sad,
All those who are anxious or are afraid.
Especially we think of (names).

We wish them well;
We wish them joy;
We wish them peace.

When someone has died
(name) has died;
Leaving people who love (her),
Leaving people who grieve,
Leaving people who feel lost and lonely.
(name) has lived:
Giving and receiving love,
Knowing and enjoying friendship.
We give thanks for (her) life;
We give thanks for all that (she) meant to us.

When a baby has been born
We welcome baby (name) into the world;
We wish (him) health and happiness;
We wish (him) the love of family and friends.
Baby (name), we are happy you are born.
Baby (name), we welcome you.

Welcoming new members of the school
We welcome you into our school.
We look forward to learning with you;
We look forward to laughing with you.
May you be a blessing to us;
May we be a blessing to you.
(Name), we welcome you.

Hearing Good News
Good news! Good news!
We give thanks for this good news.
(Add a line here describing the news, for example, 'Mrs Smith is home from hospital,' or 'A peace treaty was signed yesterday')
Let's be glad, let us shout,
Good news! Good news!
(Follow this with a round of applause).

A Hindu prayer for teacher and students
This is adapted from the Kenopanishad, part of the Hindu scriptures. The teacher and student would recite it together before beginning to study:
May we both work safely.
May both enjoy our work.
May we both work hard together.
May our study light our way.
May we not dispute with each other.
Peace, peace, peace.

CHAPTER 2

History

Stories from the past can be a valuable source for the focus of school worship, and the content of the History National Curriculum invites many questions to do with value and belief. However, whereas in the classroom history lesson the emphasis is on the objective reconstruction of what people valued and believed, in worship the use of the past is to speak to the needs of the present. To understand this, consideration must be given to the mainstream Christian view of history.

Christianity is a historical religion, in two ways. The faith rests on the historical figure of Jesus, with the belief that what he said and did has significance for humanity today. However, the place of history in the Christian faith is not confined to the story of Jesus. The faith of the Jews, from which Christianity was born, views history in terms of the working out of God's purposes and God's plan: history is seen not just as a secular study, but as a religious study too.

BACKGROUND

Christianity has maintained this tradition in the New Testament. Christians believe that the people and events of the Bible, and the people and events of history have something to say to the present.

This is most clearly seen in the Holy Communion service or Mass, which is itself an act of remembrance at the heart of Christian worship. In this service the breaking of bread and sharing of wine, which Jesus performed at the Last Supper, is re-enacted. This makes a historical event present and significant to the participant.

The significance of the past is also evident in the use of the Scriptures in church, both the

readings and sermons, and in the pictures and stained-glass windows. Nor is this use of the past restricted to the Bible; saints, church councils and ancient liturgies all have their part to play in making the events of the past relevant to the present.

In incorporating historical stories into a book on worship, we are upholding the place of history in worship, and sustaining the view that the past can speak to the present. Of course, the telling of these stories has been shaped by our twentieth-century preconceptions and our perceptions of children's needs and concerns. Our objective has not been to build up accurate historical accounts, because our task has been a theological not a historical one. Nevertheless, we have sought to be faithful to the sources and, where we have expanded the tale for the sake of a 'good story', to be coherent with them.

We have not, we hope, turned these events of the past into morality tales. Instead our intention is that they should challenge the children and give them new perceptions and something to think about. They should raise questions of value and belief which could be followed up in classroom discussion; not leave the child smugly righteous, guilty or fearful, as morality tales often do. Sometimes they may even leave the child inspired. There are, however, some recurring themes which run through them: slavery and freedom, responsibility, bravery, fear, ambivalence. These could provide a series on a thematic rather than a historical basis. Although there are many Christians represented in this section, there are also people of other faiths and none. Our comments in the introduction on non-Christian material in worship apply here. Theologically one can argue that the spirit of God has not been confined to the Church, that in all ages Jews and Christians have seen God's hand moving outside the body of believers, and have learned from their encounters with other faiths. So it is fitting that within an act of worship children should listen to voices from a non-Christian as well as a Christian past.

The stories are linked to the History Study Units of the National Curriculum but are by no means a definitive list of what could be used in connection with each unit.

1. Something old

Assembly type
Infant assembly involving classroom activity.

What you need
An object you treasure which you have had a long time (such as a toy, a piece of jewellery, a book, a picture, or even a piece of kitchen equipment such as an efficient potato peeler), modelling clay or drawing materials.

What to do
This assembly could take place in one session or be spread over a couple of days.

Show the children the object and tell them its story, explaining why you treasure it. This might be because you've grown to love it, or because it reminds you of the person who gave it to you, or simply because it makes life simpler for you. If there has been an occasion when you thought you had lost it, tell the children about it and describe your feelings at the time.

Ask the children to make a model or drawing of something which is precious to them and which they have had for a long time. Discuss with them the range of objects they might include. Alternatively ask them to bring in the object from home to continue the session the next day. This, of course, has the attendant risk that their objects are either too valued to bring to school, or will get lost.

Another introduction to this assembly would be to use the book *Dogger* by Shirley Hughes which has the same underlying theme.

Later that day or a following day, invite some of the children to talk about their pictures or models in a short time of worship. Tell the other children that theirs will be made available for the others to see either in a display or in a class book.

Prayer/reflection
Ask the children to shut their eyes and think about an object which is very precious to them.

Say, 'Let us give thanks for the things we have had a long time and treasure because they give us joy.'

Then invite the children to show their thanks by giving a big clap.

Song/hymn
Come and Praise
4 Autumn days
32 Thank you, Lord (adapting the words to your chosen objects)
57 Lost and found

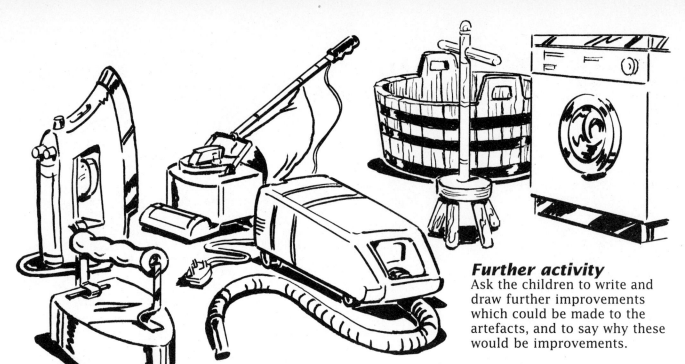

2. Getting better all the time?

Assembly type

A classroom-based assembly which could be used with all ages, although it is directly linked with the Programme of Study for History KS1. It also has links with Technology and the cross-curricular theme of economic awareness. It should be an assembly which raises questions rather than imposes answers.

What you need

Old, clearly out-dated objects and their modern counterparts (pictures or models could be used). Objects could include an old flat iron and a modern steam one; a heavy old camera and a modern 'instant' one; a boiler and mangle and a washing machine and spin dryer; an early car and a recent one; a scroll and a book.

What to do

Ask the children to list the obvious differences between the old and new artefacts and to think about which one would be easier to use and why. Ask them to think about why manufacturers and individual inventors strive to improve goods. Talk about whether the new versions are always better, and the fact that sometimes in the past things lasted longer and were more reliable than today because now there is often built-in obsolescence. With older children, raise the issue of manufacturers creating dissatisfaction so as to create a market.

Prayer/reflection

Ask the children to think about the work of those trying to improve objects because they really want life to be easier for customers.

Song

Play a recording of the Beatles' song 'Getting better all the time', and invite the children to join in.

Further activity

Ask the children to write and draw further improvements which could be made to the artefacts, and to say why these would be improvements.

3. What has changed?

Assembly type

A classroom-based infant assembly.

What you need

A visit from a person aged over 50 (such as a member of staff, or a child's relative).

What to do

Introduce the visitor to the children, then brainstorm together a list of all the things which are commonplace in British society today and which either were not invented or had very restricted use when the guest was a child (for example computers, microwave ovens, cassette players, dishwashers, felt-tipped pens and videos). However, remember to point out that not everyone has these things in their homes, even if they can afford them. Then pose the question of whether children have changed that much.

Ask your guest to talk about generalised activities in the home. For example, she didn't play on computers, but some of the games she played would be similar to ones played today. Some of the kitchen equipment is different but the purpose, that of providing food, is still the same. Encourage her to talk about helping in the home, quarrelling and playing with siblings and other similar, normal family activities.

Prayer/reflection
Ask the children to think of one thing which they are glad has changed since the visitor was small, one thing which they are glad has remained the same and one thing which they are sorry has remained the same.

Further activity
Read *Peepo!* by Allan and Janet Ahlberg. How do the pictures of home life shown in the book differ from the home life of the children?

4. The photograph album

Assembly type
Classroom-based infant assembly.

What you need
Grandma's Bill by Martin Waddell.

What to do
Read the book to the children, and ask them to express their feelings about it. They may wish to comment about the death of a grandparent or great-grandparent. Ask them whether they thought the grandmother liked looking at the photos and why, and whether they like looking at photos from the past and why. Comment on the value of photos to record experiences and bring back memories of the past.

Prayer/reflection
Ask the children to shut their eyes and think about something happy from the past or somebody special whom they don't see anymore.

Further activities
Ask the children each to bring in a photo which is special, either because it reminds them of somebody special or because it shows a happy occasion. Help them caption the pictures to make a display. Alternatively, let the children draw 'photos' which they wish they had. Start a photo album about the class.

5. Diogenes and Alexander

Assembly type
An all-age assembly linked to SU 4, Ancient Greece.

What you need
Copy of photocopiable page 136.

What to do
Read the assembly story on page 136 or tell it in your own words. It doesn't need an introduction.

Prayer/reflection
Listen to these words of John Bunyan:

He that is down need fear no fall,
    He that is low no pride;
    He that is humble ever shall have
    God to be his guide.

    I am content with what I have,
    little be it or much;
    and, Lord, contentment still I crave, because thou savest such.

Song/hymn
Ancient and Modern (New Standard Version)
218 He that is down need fear no fall (a setting of the above words)
Come and Praise
97 Simple gifts ('Tis the gift to be simple)

Further activities
• Discuss with the children why Alexander might have envied Diogenes.
• Ask them to write a story about a time when they felt happy and content.

6. What have the Romans ever done for us?

Assembly type
Junior assembly linked to SU 1, Romans, Anglo-Saxons and Vikings in Britain.

What you need
Map of the world or the Middle East, a copy of photocopiable page 137.

What to do
Imperialism inevitably raises the question of whether invaders bring anything of worth to their colonies. The following story looks at the issue with regard to the Romans in Palestine, but has application to any situation of conquest including the Romans in Britain. This retelling of a tale in the Talmud is heavily influenced by the film *Monty Python's Life of Brian* and indeed it is possible that the scriptwriters were familiar with the original, although the conclusion reached is quite different. The scene from the film could be used in the classroom follow-up to compare endings, but bear in mind that it is of a controversial nature.

Begin by commenting to the children how hard it must be to have foreigners ruling your country. Tell them that the Romans not only invaded and occupied England, they also occupied many other countries including Palestine. Show the children the map and point out Palestine. Then read the assembly story on page 137 or tell it in your own words.

Further activities
• Discuss whether Rabbi Simeon was right or wrong to reject the idea that the Romans had done something for Palestine. Can others benefit from the selfish desires of a few? Is free speech important? Should people be allowed to speak their views on the government?
• As part of the children's study of the Roman invasion of Britain, help them write the same story in a British context.

7. Refugees

Assembly type
Teacher-led assembly for juniors linked to SU 1, Romans, Anglo-Saxons and Vikings in Britain.

What you need
Pictures of refugees in crowded hostels or camps, copy of photocopiable page 138.

What to do
The language used in the quotations from St Jerome on page 138 is fairly difficult, but an accurate translation gives a better flavour of the style than too much simplification.

Show the pictures to the children and explain what is happening in them. Then adapt the assembly story on page 138 as appropriate.

Prayer/reflection
We think about refugees from wars in all parts of the world today. May there always be people ready to give up what they are doing in order to help.

Song/hymn
Come and Praise
65 When I needed a neighbour
70 Cross over the road

8. Caedmon

Assembly type
Teacher-led junior assembly linked with SU 1, Romans, Anglo-Saxons and Vikings in Britain.

What you need
Copy of photocopiable pages 139 to 141.

What to do
Adapt the story on pages 139 to 141 to your own style.

Prayer/reflection
Ask the children to close their eyes and think of something that they would like to be good at. Say, 'Sometimes we are sad that we cannot do things as well as we would like. May all of us find a gift, a talent, or a skill that we can develop.'

Song/hymn
Come and Praise
13 Song of Caedmon
64 The wise may bring their learning

9. King Alfred's book

Assembly type
Teacher-led assembly linked to SU 1, Romans, Anglo-Saxons and Vikings in Britain.

What you need
A selection of favourite passages of your own that you might collect in a book, a scrapbook, adhesive, copy of photocopiable pages 142 to 143.

What to do
Before the assembly, prepare a scrapbook containing some of your favourite poems and passages. Ask one of the children to take on the role of Asser and let him rehearse his reading several times before

10. Tudor times

the assembly. Adapt the assembly story on pages 142 to 143 if necessary.

Next read two or three of your own favourite passages from your scrapbook. Emphasise that you have chosen them just because you like them. If you or anyone you know does keep such a book, show it to the children.

Player/reflection
Read again one of the passages that you have chosen, and invite the children to say 'Amen' if they agree with the idea expressed.

Song/hymn
Come and Praise
72 A living song

Further activity
Encourage the children to select passages, from as wide-ranging sources as possible, and copy them into their own 'handbooks'.

Assembly type
Junior assembly linked to SU 2, Life in Tudor times and to SU 6, A past non-European society. It could also be linked with assemblies 17 and 18 in the Geography section, in challenging a Euro-centric view of the world.

What you need
Copies of photocopiable pages 144 and 145 and props to represent a 'time machine'. (This could be as simple as a chair, in which the 'time traveller' mimes pressing buttons, or you could let your imagination run riot!)

Preparation
This assembly is designed to give a different slant on the study of 'Life in Tudor times'.

Prepare the dialogue for the countries and events that you are going to cover. Brief one child to act as the 'time traveller' and others to take on other roles as appropriate.

Choose a more able reader to read the passages describing sixteenth-century Benin.

As this idea works best when the area is likely to be unfamiliar to the children, we have given a dialogue that introduces the Mogul Empire of Akbar in North-Western India. The same idea could be used in connection with the West African kingdom of Benin, which is included as one of the possible areas of study in SU 6. If you do use this area, we suggest that you do the assembly before the children are introduced to Benin.

What to do
Introduce the topic of 'Life in Tudor Times', and ask for examples of events that happened at that time. Tell the children that today they have the privilege of hearing a special report from a 'time-travelling correspondent'. The 'time traveller' then gets into the 'time machine', and indicates that he is travelling backwards in time as far as the sixteenth century. Then use the text on photocopiable pages 144 and 145.

Prayer/reflection

We have been looking at life in Britain during the reign of the Tudor kings and queens when there were many great and powerful kingdoms and empires in the world. Many people in other parts of the world would never have heard of the Tudors and most would not have cared about what was going on in Britain.

Sometimes we think of places as being 'remote', or 'far away', and think that because of this they are less important. Let us remember that every place is important to the people who live there, and their lives matter just as much as ours.

Song/hymn

Come and Praise
19 He's got the whole world
69 The family of Man
148 Let the world rejoice together

Further activity

Prepare a time-line covering events which happened in different parts of the world during the sixteenth century. Help the children research events to put on it.

11. Reading the Bible

Assembly type

Dramatised presentation based on SU 2, Life in Tudor times.

What you need

The largest book you can find (to represent the Bible), photocopiable page 146, sixteenth-century costumes (optional) and props.

Preparation

Prepare the dramatised presentation from photocopiable page 146. The parts can be played in sixteenth-century costume, or more simply perhaps, with a few props.

The part of the 'Teacher' needs to be played by a female teacher; that of the 'Leader' needs to be a male teacher or a boy if he is able to convey clearly such a large speaking part. The other 'walk-on' parts can be played by the children.

What to do

Introduce the topic of Tudor times, and talk about some of the events and areas the children have studied. Remind them that it was a time of great religious argument and discussion, with many new things happening and new ideas being expressed. Then use the dramatised text on page 146.

Tell the children that much has changed since the sixteenth century, but it took a long time before women were allowed to read the Bible in church. Nowadays, in this country, people have the right to read whatever they like, but it has not always been so, and it is not so in some countries even today.

Prayer/reflection

Let us never take for granted the privilege of finding things out for ourselves by reading. Let us give thanks that we have schools and books to help us.

Song/hymn

Come and Praise
67 Black and white
72 A living song

Further activity
Ask the children to research some different translations of the Bible, and find out when and why they were produced.

12. Lancashire and the USA civil war

Assembly type
Dramatised junior assembly linked with SU 3a, Victorian Britain.

What you need
Map of the world to show the routes of cotton and slave ships, picture of Abraham Lincoln (optional), some raw cotton and some spun cotton, copies of photocopiable pages 147 and 148.

Preparation
Prepare different children to say or read the roles of the cotton workers in the meeting. Rehearse the others to act as people at the meeting.

As a backdrop to the drama, prepare a display using some raw cotton and some spun cotton, a map of the world and a picture of Abraham Lincoln if you have one.

What to do
Ask the children if there are any local monuments that they have noticed. Who are they of?

What are they about? Follow this by using the material on photocopiable pages 147 and 148.

Prayer/reflection
Let us remember and give thanks for all those who struggled against slavery: the slaves themselves, the people who fought and died and the workers in England who were prepared to go hungry rather than support the system of slavery. Let us remember too the injustices that people suffer today. May we be prepared to give up things we like if it will help to make a fairer world.

(You could mention some injustices that you think the children may know about: poverty, unfair trade, oppression in different parts of the world.)

Song/hymn

We shall overcome
Come and Praise
71 If I had a hammer
Alleluya! (A & C Black) A Negro spiritual (this book is just one source and contains several spirituals about freedom).

Further activities

Teach the children some Negro spirituals. Tell them more about the conditions in the cotton fields, and help them find out about the conditions of the cotton workers in this country.

Use this information to help them set up an imaginary correspondence between an American slave and an English cotton worker. Help them research into the abolition of slavery in this country. Using materials from the Anti-Slavery Society (See Resources, page 192), tell the children about modern forms of slavery.

13. Reports from the Front

Assembly type

Junior assembly linking with SU 3a, Victorian Britain.

What you need

A copy of one of the day's newspapers, a world map, copy of photocopiable page 149.

What to do

Show the children a daily newspaper and read the headlines from war zones.

Point out the appropriate places on the map. Then go on to say that today you will be talking about the newspaper reports of a war which took place over a hundred years ago when Queen Victoria reigned.

Read the assembly text on page 149 or adapt it in your own style.

Prayer/reflection

We give thanks for the work of men and women who are willing to risk their lives reporting wars. We pray for the safety of those covering wars in [insert the name of a location currently in the news] at this very time.

Song/hymn

Come and Praise
142 Down by the riverside

Further activities

• Help the children find out more about the life of Florence Nightingale.
• Research with the children accounts of the Crimean war, and try to build up a picture of the life of a soldier.
• Help the children to work through newspapers collating a list of war correspondents and where they are.

14. Coventry Cathedral

Assembly type

Junior assembly linked to SU 3b, Britain since 1930.

What you need

Map of England, pictures of Coventry Cathedral, a candle, copy of photocopiable pages 150 to 151.

What to do

Show the children where Coventry is on the map of England and then let them look at pictures of the old and new cathedrals.

Adapt the assembly story on pages 150 to 151 to your own style.

Prayer/reflection

Light a candle and ask the children to think of the way war hurts and destroys people's lives. Invite the children to pray with you for all those who work for peace.

Further activities
• Discuss with the children what they think working for peace means. Help the children to find out more about the reconciliation work based at Coventry Cathedral and about others who work for peace.
• Ask the children to design stained-glass windows with a symbol of peace and forgiveness in them.

15. Building a church –1

Assembly type
The first of two consecutive junior assemblies. The first assembly is based on junior class work based around a local parish church. The work could be linked to SU 5, Local History, and possibly another one of the SUs, depending upon the age of the church being studied.

Stage 1 – Preparation

What you need
Access to your parish church, church guide book, local history books, pens, paper, drawing and painting materials.

What to do
Research with the children the origins of a local church, considering not only when it was built but why it was built. A common reason is population growth, but it can also be that a particular denomination has increased in size in the area. Look at where the building materials came from, what skills were needed and who the labourers were.

Consider with the children why the people would have wanted a church, emphasising the importance of faith.

Prepare the material for presentation in an assembly in any of the following ways.
• Ask the children to make large illustrations of the workmen and people at the time and of what the land might have looked like before the building. Ask the children to be prepared to talk about their pictures.
• Ask the children to prepare a series of short dramatic scenes illustrating the history of the building of the church.
• Encourage the class to write imaginary diaries of the various people involved in the building of the church, for example the architect, the stonemason, the plumber and the vicar at the time.

Stage 2 – Assembly

What you need
Children's work, costumes for drama.

What to do
Ask the children to present the work they have prepared.

Prayer/reflection
Let us remember those people who built the church. Some built it because it was just a job to do and they needed the money. Some built it because they wanted to make a place for people to pray and worship God. Let us remember those people who paid for the building of the church. Some paid for it because they wanted others to think that they were generous. Some paid for it because they wanted a place for people to pray and worship God. Whatever the motive, whatever the reason, we give thanks that they built it and paid for it.

Song/hymn
Come and Praise
61 The building song

Further activity
Ask the children to design their own modern church, thinking about what they would put in it, and considering the purpose of a church.

16. Building a church – 2

Assembly type
Junior assembly, to follow on from the previous one. This could be linked to SU 3b, Britain since 1930.

What you need
Copy of photocopiable page 152.

What to do
Remind the children of the previous assembly and then adapt the assembly story on page 152 to your own style.

Prayer/reflection
Ask the children to think about something they have been proud of because they have made or helped to make it.

Song/hymn
Come and Praise
61 The building song

Further activities
• Discuss the prayer/reflection with the children.
• Visit a local church with the children and identify what things the local congregation have made for the church.
• If you have close links with a local church, make a gift for it.

This could either be something permanent, such as a banner, or a temporary display.

17. The first mosque

Assembly type
Junior assembly.

What you need
Pictures of mosques, including both purpose-built and adapted ones, copy of photocopiable page 153.

What to do
Tell or remind the children of the story of Muhammad and adapt the assembly text on page 153 to your own style.

Prayer/reflection
Ask the children to close their eyes and imagine wandering like the camel in the story, looking for a good place to sit and be quiet or to meet with other people. What would their place be like? Who would they like to meet there? What thoughts and prayers would they have there?

CHAPTER 3

Geography

Geographical topics can be the basis of worship in several different ways. First of all there is the concept of the holy place. Christianity, in common with other major faiths, teaches that God is everywhere and can be worshipped everywhere. Yet Christianity has its holy places, both buildings set aside or built for worship, and places which are holy because of their association with Jesus or a saint. Worship in school can encourage children to reflect on the places which are holy or special in their lives.

Secondly, there is the question of responsibility. Who owns the land? Who is responsible for it? These are key religious questions which children can begin to think about at this stage.

Thirdly, the weather, the study of which is an essential component of the Geography National Curriculum, is also something which forms part of religious tradition and dialogue. The ancient Old Testament ideas of the weather being a sign of God's pleasure or anger are, we believe, inappropriate to the context of school worship where there is no opportunity for debate. However, for children to think about their relationship to the weather is part of the process of exploring where they see themselves as fitting into the natural world. Being aware of the consequences of bad weather is also part of that process. In this chapter, we use the example of the wind, but one could base similar assemblies on the sun or the rain.

Lastly, the language of geography can have a metaphorical function in faith. For example, the journey of life is an idea which is found in many faiths and traditions, and which expresses clearly the sense of moving on, often in the face of difficulty, which is experienced by both adults and children.

1. Holy places

Assembly type
School assembly on a theme of place and history and buildings, connecting with the study of places, and with the thematic study of settlement.

What you need
A picture of Makkah, a picture of a mosque.

What to do
This and the following assembly focus on a theme of place and history and buildings. This first assembly is particularly appropriate at the time of the Hajj (a movable feast, fixed according to the appearance of the new moon), the mass Muslim pilgrimage to Makkah in Saudi Arabia.

Tell the children that once a year Muslims travel from all over the world to the holy city of Makkah. They go to obey some words in the Qur'an, their holy book, which says they should try to make this pilgrimage at least once in a lifetime. Makkah is such a holy place that only Muslims are allowed to visit it and when they go on pilgrimage they must all wear white clothes to show they are all equal in God's sight. Muslims believe that the first house on earth was built by Adam in Makkah.

Makkah is such a holy place for Muslims that when they pray they face Makkah. In the mosques the wall facing Makkah is called the 'qiblah' wall. When Muslims go to the mosque to pray they face the qiblah wall.

Although Makkah is a very holy place, Muslims believe that God is everywhere and that you can pray to him anywhere. They say that the whole world is a mosque, a place to pray. The whole world is holy.

Prayer/reflection
Listen to these words from the Qur'an about Makkah:

> Remember We made the House
> A place of assembly for men
> And a place of safety;
> And take ye the Station
> Of Abraham as a place of prayer.
> (Sura 2:125)

Now shut your eyes and think about the whole world as a holy place.

Song/hymn
Come and Praise
97 Simple gifts ('Tis the gift to be simple)

2. Making a holy place

Assembly type
School assembly on a theme of place and history and buildings, connecting with the study of places, and with the thematic study of settlement.

What you need
Prayer mat, pictures showing the inside of churches and mosques.

What to do
Remind the children that Muslims have a holy place to which they travel on pilgrimage, and that they go to mosques to pray with other Muslims. Tell them that the insides of mosques are often very beautiful with fine writing and intricate patterns on the walls; representational art is prohibited. Muslims want to make their mosques into special places, just as Christians want their churches to be special places. Look with the children at the ways in which a church or mosque may be made beautiful. Tell them that Muslims do not only pray at the mosque. They must pray at least five times a day and are often at home or work when it is prayer time. As they want to make their prayer place a special place, a holy place, different to their normal surroundings, they use a prayer mat.

Prayer/reflection
Listen to these words which Muslims pray every day, often when they are kneeling on their prayer mats. Remember that Allah is the Muslim name for God.

All praise is for Allah, the Lord of the Universe, the most merciful, the most Kind: Master of the day of judgement. You alone do we worship, from you alone we seek help.
(Qur'an, Sura 1:1-5; translation from *The Children's Book of Salah* by Ghulam Sarwar.)

Song/hymn
Come and Praise
41 Fill thou my life

Further activity
Discuss with the children the ways in which people make a room attractive and a pleasant place to be.

3. Too much weather

Assembly type
Junior assembly for the class or to be presented by one class to the whole school.

Stage 1 – Preparation

What you need
Musical instruments, local or national newspapers featuring reports of heavy rain or floods, either current or in the past (for example, the gales of 16 October 1987, or flooding in North Wales in November 1989), paper, paint, pens, scissors.

What to do
Help the children prepare a 'storm' composition, using either their bodies or instruments to make the sounds.

Ask the children to research the effects of severe weather such as gales and storms on a community, using the newspapers or other resources. Help them to prepare a 'television' report on the weather conditions. They could use any or all of the following ideas.

• Indicate on a large map the place concerned and the appropriate weather symbols.
• Paint large pictures of the place and/or a backdrop showing the devastation caused.
• Write and dramatise a script for a television reporter interviewing people about the effects of the weather.

Stage 2 – Assembly

What you need
The items produced in the preparation stage.

What to do
Have the children play the 'storm' composition. Ask one child to give a 'weather report' of the place the children have studied, using the prepared map and pictures. Ask the children to act out their television report.

Prayer/reflection
Ask the children to play the 'storm' composition again, and to think or, if they like, to pray about people who have had to cope with storms and flooding.

Song/hymn
Come and Praise
74 Sad, puzzled eyes

The wind

The wind as a symbol of the Spirit or a life-giving force is a central image in Christianity. These assemblies offer the opportunity to explore that image experientially as well as affirming the place of the wind in creation.

4. Whistling wind

Assembly type
Class assembly for five to nine year olds.

What you need
Cassette recorder or record-player, recordings of music evoking the breeze, a copy of *The Wind Blew* by Pat Hutchins, copy of photocopiable page 154.

What to do
Play a selection of music to the children evoking breezes and light winds. Read the two wind poems by Christina Rossetti on page 154. Read together *The Wind Blew* by Pat Hutchins, encouraging the children to anticipate each page before you read it.

Prayer/reflection
Listen again to the music.

5. Creatures of the wind

Assembly type
Class assembly for lower juniors.

What you need
Copy of photocopiable page 155.

What to do
Remind the children that you've been thinking about the wind; that you can't see the wind, you can only see where it has been and hear what it moves. Introduce the idea of seeing the wind as being like a person, an animal or an object. How would the children draw it?

Read the poem by RL Stevenson on page 155. Read it again, encouraging the children to imitate the wind as a galloping horseman.

Ask them to suggest other animals or sorts of people of which the wind reminds them.

Further activity
Ask the children to draw the wind as a person or an animal.

6. Needing the wind

Assembly type
Class or whole-school assembly for all ages.

What you need
The story 'Hanuman the child of the wind' in *A Tapestry of Tales* by Sandra Palmer and Elizabeth Breuilly.

What to do
Read the story of 'Hanuman the child of the wind' or tell it in your own words. Ask the children for comment.

Ask them to sit quietly and think about:
• the sun being annoyed by the monkey;
• the wind god weeping for the loss of his son;
• the people with no crops;
• Indra realising he had made a mistake;
• the monkey god restored to life;
• the people having food again.

7. Wind images

Assembly type
Assembly to be given by one class to the whole school or other classes.

Stage 1 – Preparation

What you need
A cassette recorder and some 'wind' music (for example, Mendelssohn's *Fingal's Cave* Overture, Beethoven's Symphony No. 6, Grieg's *Peer Gynt*), paints, paper, felt-tipped pens, pictures and book illustrations depicting the wind, percussion instruments.

What to do
In a dance lesson, explain to the children that they are going to make up a dance about the wind. Encourage them to consider how the wind

moves and whether it is always the same. Use the music to help them develop an understanding of the contrast between wild, stormy winds and soft, gentle breezes. Let them sit and listen to the music and, in between each movement, encourage them to picture how they would paint the various winds. Ask them to pretend to be objects tossed about by different sorts of winds and devise an appropriate dance, for example a balloon, a sheet of newspaper, an umbrella or a handkerchief. Back in the classroom, ask the children to paint a picture of the wind, encouraging them to convey a feeling of movement in the picture. Afterwards, show them pictures which demonstrate how a variety of artists have represented the wind in their paintings, including book illustrators.

In a different session, recap on your discussions about how the wind moves and how strong it can be, and also the various images of the wind. Ask the children to think about how the wind can make them feel, and how it can be exciting and frightening at the same time. Help them to remember to differentiate between the different types of wind, then together make a class 'poem' about the wind in which you record images, feelings and descriptions. Let the children compose a percussion accompaniment for the poem.

Stage 2 – Assembly

What you need
A cassette player, your chosen wind music (see Preparation), the children's wind pictures, percussion instruments.

What to do
Display the children's wind pictures and play the music as the children come in to the assembly.

Ask a group of children to recite their class wind poem, either in unison or one line per child, while others provide a music and dance accompaniment.

Prayer/reflection
Read John 3:8.

Song/hymn
Alleluya! 77 songs for thinking people
31 Blowing in the wind

Making maps

This is a series of assemblies exploring map-making. Maps are available which show the relationship between places and other variables such as politics, population and weather. The following suggestions will help children to develop an understanding of the relationship between place and value and belief. This relationship is most evident in the presence of sacred places throughout the world to which people make pilgrimage, but is also important in its secular forms.

8. What's at the centre of your world?

Assembly type
Infant assembly preceded by a classroom activity.

Stage 1 – Preparation

What you need
Copies of photocopiable page 156, pencils or felt-tipped pens.

What to do
Discuss with the children which is the most important place in their lives. (The majority, if not all, will say their homes.) Then discuss with them other places which are important to them, encouraging a wide variety of examples so that they don't just copy the first suggestion offered. Places could include school, a childminder's home, an absentee parent's home, the swimming pool, a place of worship, a friend's home or the park.

Finally, ask the children to fill in their 'map' of important places on photocopiable page 156. Encourage them to put the most important one at the centre.

Stage 2 – Assembly

What you need
The children's maps (see Preparation), display materials.

What to do
Before the assembly, make a display of the children's maps.

Invite each child to talk about her own map and why the places are important.

Prayer/reflection
We give thanks for all the places which are important to us.

Song/hymn
Come and Praise
47 One more step along the world I go
97 Simple gifts ('Tis the gift to be simple)

9. Imaginary journey

Assembly type
Infant and lower junior classroom assembly.

What you need
Copy of photocopiable page 157.

What to do
Ask the children to sit on the floor in a circle with plenty of space around them. Ask them to shut their eyes and be very still but be very relaxed too.

Then adapt the assembly text on page 157 to your own style, presenting it slowly and peacefully.

Ask the children to open their eyes and sit quietly for a few seconds, remembering the place they have visited in their imagination. Ask for volunteers to tell the others about their special place.

Prayer/reflection
Let us give thanks for those places where we feel happy.

Song/hymn
I'm H.A.P.P.Y.
Come and Praise
97 Simple gifts ('Tis the gift to be simple)

Further activity
Let the children draw or paint pictures of their happy place.

10. A secret place

Assembly type
Nursery or infant classroom assembly.

What you need
Sally's Secret by Shirley Hughes.

What to do
The building of small chapels or shrines for quiet prayer is the adult, religious extension of the love many children have of building dens or finding themselves a quiet spot, even in the most topsy-turvy homes.

The book *Sally's Secret* encapsulates that pleasure. Read *Sally's Secret* and encourage the children to talk about places they like to go when they want to be by themselves and be quiet. However, emphasise that they don't have to tell everyone else about it as they may want to keep it secret.

Prayer/reflection
Close your eyes and imagine you have that nice feeling of being in your special quiet place.

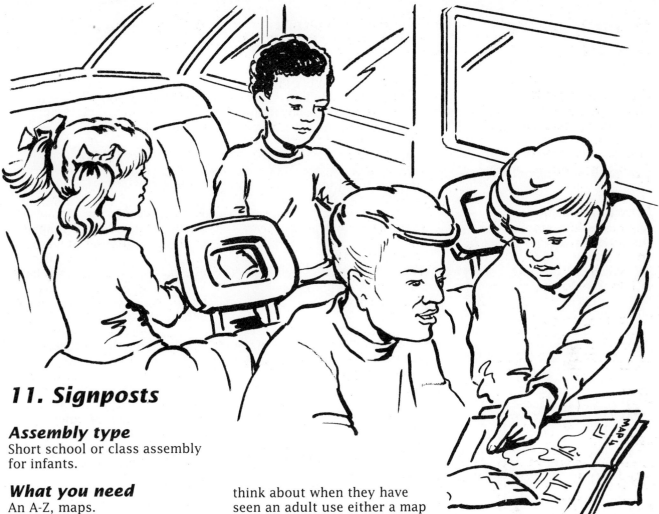

11. Signposts

Assembly type
Short school or class assembly for infants.

What you need
An A-Z, maps.

What to do
Having a sense of belonging to a place is important for all children. It is, therefore, not surprising that 'home' is a core religious symbol as the word captures the sense of belonging and not being a stranger. One characteristic of being 'at home' in a place is that you don't need maps, because you are familiar with the landmarks. Many children of this age may have difficulty in naming buildings with which they are familiar visually, but the assembly may prompt them to learn to identify them.

Show the children the maps and the A-Z and ask them to think about when they have seen an adult use either a map or an A-Z in the car. Lead them to realise that you don't need a map when you know where you are going and you don't need a map when you are near home.

Ask them to close their eyes and imagine they are on a car or bus journey coming back home. What buildings will they see which will tell them that they are near home? Suggest some of the local landmarks to them as well as the fact that they might spot a friend's house.

Try to evoke in them a memory of the feeling of being near home once more.

Then ask them to open their eyes and tell you about any buildings or landmarks near their homes.

Prayer/reflection
When we are near home, we see the things we know.
When we are near home, we hear the sounds we know.
When we are near home, we smell the smells we know.
We give thanks for the things that tell us, 'Nearly home now'.

Song/hymn
Come and Praise
97 Simple gifts ('Tis the gift to be simple)
103 I am planting my feet

10. My guide book

Assembly type
Classroom activity, possibly over several sessions, followed by a junior assembly.

Stage 1 – Preparation

What you need
Paper, scissors, stapler, pens, a guide book to act as an example.

What to do
Talk to the children in general terms about having visitors from another country, and how they might show the visitors round the area, pointing out places of interest and telling the visitors stories relating to the places. Introduce the idea of a guide book and show the children an example. Ask them to make guide books of their own lives, with pages covering the following aspects:
• where I live;
• my school;
• going shopping;
• where I meet my friends.

Stage 2 – Assembly

What you need
Personal guide books (see Preparation).

What to do
Ask some of the children to read excerpts from their guide books and make the others' books available for general reading.

Footsteps

The following three assemblies continue the theme of 'maps' and should ideally be used consecutively.

13. Famous footsteps

Assembly type
A classroom activity followed by junior assembly.

Stage 1 – Preparation

What you need
Copies of photocopiable page 158, paper, pencils, felt-tipped pens, maps of the world, biographies of famous people at the reading level of the children in your class. (If you want to restrict the children's choice, you will also need a list of people. Some people you might consider are: Muhammad, Moses, Ghandi, Emmeline Pankhurst and Elizabeth Fry. Alternatively choose people from the historical period the class is currently studying.)

What to do

Giving thanks for someone's example, while accepting their faults, is part of the heritage of the Christian and other faiths.

Talk to the children about the idea of going on a journey to follow in the footsteps of a famous person, visiting the places where they were born, lived, worked and died. For example, every year people visit Israel to follow in the footsteps of Jesus, visiting Bethlehem, Nazareth, Bethany and Jerusalem. Others follow in the footsteps of St Paul.

Ask the children to research, either individually or in pairs, the life of someone of their own choice, or someone from the list you provide, by finding out about the places in that person's life. Ask the children to present their findings pictorially on the 'footsteps map' on photocopiable page 158 and then write a commentary about it. Older or more able children could write an imaginary diary as though they were following in the chosen person's footsteps.

Stage 2 – Assembly

What you need
No special equipment.

What to do
Ask the children to tell the rest of the class about the person whose footsteps they have traced, describing any journeys they made. Allow several sessions for this if necessary.

Prayer/reflection
We give thanks for the life of.... Amen.

14. Following in my footsteps

Assembly type
Classroom activity followed by junior classroom assembly.

Stage 1 – Preparation

What you need
Copies of photocopiable page 158, pencils, felt-tipped pens.

What to do
Suggest to the children that they might one day become famous. What places would someone want to visit if they

were following in the children's footsteps? Are there any places that the children know are important to them but someone else might not know about? Ask them to do a 'footsteps' map of their own lives, using photocopiable page 158.

Stage 2 – Assembly

What you need
The 'footsteps' maps, display materials.

What to do
Ask the children to talk about their footsteps maps. This may need several sessions.

At the end, put the maps on display.

Prayer/reflection
We give thanks for all our lives.

15. Who did you follow?

Assembly type
Junior class assembly for the whole school, based on the two previous assemblies.

Stage 1 – Preparation

What you need
Paint, large pieces of paper, large pieces of card, pens.

What to do
Divide the class into groups to work on different aspects of the assembly.
• Ask one group of children to turn their research material into a dialogue presentation. The following is one possible format:
Child 1: Why are you looking so exhausted?
Child 2: I've been following in the footsteps of...
Child 3: Who is she?
Child 2: She was...
Child 1: Where did you go?

(Child 2 then recounts the chosen person's life story.)
• Ask another group to paint large scenes of the relevant places, and put them behind windows cut from card, so that the scenes can be revealed at the appropriate moment. Have these on display for the school assembly.
• Ask the rest of the children to work in pairs to write prayers giving thanks for places the children cherish.

Stage 2 – Assembly

What you need
'Window' display (see Preparation).

What to do
Have the children enact their 'play' or 'plays' making use of the display to emphasise the importance of places.

Song/hymn
Come and Praise
47 One more step along the world I go

Prayer/reflection
Let the children read the prayers they have composed.

16. Feelings map

Assembly type
Classroom activity followed by junior classroom assembly.

Stage 1 – Preparation

What you need
Maps of the area near the school, paper, pencils.

What to do
This assembly activity depends on the children being familiar with their own local area, and with maps of it.

Distribute maps of the local area and ask the children to mark in familiar landmarks. Then ask them to work out a 'feelings' colour code with which to shade their maps, showing, for example, places they like to linger, places they like to hurry through and places they see as dangerous.

Ask the children to try to express their reactions to the different places in the form of a short description or poem.

Stage 2 – Assembly

What you need
Poems and maps (see Preparation).

What to do
Before the assembly, make a display of the children's maps. Bring the group together. Invite the children to read out their poems and show their maps.

Prayer/reflection
In the places where we like to linger,
May we find peace.
In the places where we are afraid,
May we be kept safe.
In the places where we are happy,
May we be thankful.
(You could add similar lines for any other feelings that the children have indicated.)

17. Which way up?

Assembly type
Short junior assembly.

What you need
A conventional map of the world. a map of the world with Antarctica and Australia in the top half (for example, the 'Down Under map of the World', see Resources page 192) pins, notice board.

What to do
It is easy for children (and adults) to take it for granted that the Northern Hemisphere must always be at the top of the map. Learning that some things are symbolic

conventions rather than actual realities is part of religious development. The assembly will be difficult conceptually for many children, but the objective is not to increase scientific understanding, but to increase wonder at the complexity of creation and to learn to question conventions (a part of the Christian prophetic tradition).

Unroll the map of the world and ask the children to help you to put it up on the noticeboard. Ask them which way up it should go. How do they know? Is it just the lettering that tells them? Explain to them that it is only a convention to have the map this way, that the earth is suspended in space. There is no top or bottom, and when astronauts orbit the earth, sometimes it looks to them as though Australia is at the top, and at other times it looks as though Britain is at the top.

Tell the children that some Australians are fed up with Australia always being put at the bottom of the world map, so they have started making maps which look upside down to people from the Northern Hemisphere, but the right way up to them. Put up the map with Australia at the top.

Prayer/reflection
Whichever way we look at it, the world is an amazing place. Amen.

Song/hymn
Come and Praise
19 He's got the whole world in his hands

Further activity
Using a beach ball globe as a rough guide, which can easily be held at different angles, ask the children to make maps with different countries at the top.

18. The centre of the world

Assembly type
Short junior assembly.

What you need
An ordinary compass (optional: a qiblah compass, a picture of the Ka'bah in Makkah, a picture of the Mappa Mundi, pictures of Jerusalem).

What to do
Ask the children if they know which direction they are facing. Get out the normal compass and ask a child to read it. Do the children know of any buildings in the direction they are facing?

Explain that when Muslims pray they always make sure that they are facing towards Makkah because their prophet, Muhammad, was told by God to instruct them to face that way when they pray. In Makkah is a building which Muslims believe was built by the prophet Ibrahim (whom Christians and Jews call Abraham). They believe that this was on the same site as the first building that Adam, the first man, built on earth. Most important of all, Muslims believe that if you face Makkah when you pray, it will help you

think about God and his prophets, instead of all your normal worries. Muslims believe that God should be at the centre of a person's life.

Tell the children about the Mappa Mundi, an ancient world map in Hereford cathedral, which places Jerusalem at the centre of the world. Explain that Jerusalem is a holy city for both Jews and Christians. This map, too, is saying that God should be at the centre of people's lives.

Make the point that people of different faiths have things in common and things about which they differ. Perhaps one thing they agree on, is that everyone should think about what should be at the centre of their lives.

Prayer/reflection

(Adapted from the Qur'an, Sura 2:148)

Each one has a goal to which God turns him. So strive together, as if you were in a race, towards all that is good. Wherever you are, God will bring you together. For God has power over all things.

The land and Australian Aboriginals

Although the subject of this series of assemblies is a far-away remote place, remote even from the lives of most Australian children who live in the coastal area, it nevertheless links in with a study on the local area and land use because it encourages children to think about their own physical surroundings including their responsibilities towards it.

19. The land

Assembly type

Teacher-led assembly for all ages.

What you need

Optional (use some or all of the following): a large map showing political boundaries, a 'For Sale' sign, mock land deeds, a map of Australia, pictures of the first English settlers of Australia, Australian Aboriginals and Australian animals, copy of photocopiable page 159.

What to do

Although some of the concepts in this assembly are quite difficult, the basic idea of ownership is one that can be grasped and thought about by even quite young children.

Talk to the children about buying a house, and how the lawyers have to sort out who owns the property. Talk about the sort of problem that can sometimes happen where there is disputed territory, for example concerning shared driveways, and how people put up fences to divide off one person's property from the next.

Move on to telling the children about the English settlers going to Australia, adapting the assembly text on page 159 to your own words.

In the Bible there is a similar idea, 'The earth is the Lord's, and everything in it' (Psalm 24:1a, New International Version). The people on earth can look after and enjoy the land, but it doesn't really belong to them.

Prayer/reflection

Invite the children to listen to this Aboriginal statement about the land:

> To us, the land is a living thing
> The land is our mother

It is the source of our existence
Our religion, our identity
To us land is a living thing,
We are part of it
And it is a part of us.
(taken from *Liturgy of Life* by Donald Hilton.)

Song/hymn

Come and Praise
6 The earth is yours, O God

Further activity

Ask the children to consider and discuss the following questions.
• What land in this country belongs to everyone and is everyone's duty to look after?
• Can we do what we like with land?
• What things damage the land?

20. Why is the land precious?

Assembly type

Teacher-led assembly for all ages. (The discussion questions, however, are more suitable for older children.)

What you need

A map of Australia, a picture of an Australian Aboriginal, sample rocks or pictures of rocks, something made of gold, copy of photocopiable page 160.

What to do

Show the children the item made of gold, and encourage them to comment on how precious it is. Ask them where gold is found (that is underground), how it is got from the ground and what other precious things lie under the ground which make the land very valuable. Then adapt the assembly text on page 160 to your own style, or alternatively tell the children about the arguments over mineral resources in Antarctica.

Song/hymn
Come and Praise
16 When God made the garden of creation
76 God in his love for us lent us this planet

Prayer/reflection
Sit quietly and think about a place which is important to you.

Further activity
Ask the children to consider, research and discuss the following questions.
• Are there any sacred sites used for religious ceremonies locally?
• What other things make land valuable?
• What places are important to the children?

21. Visiting other people's sacred sites

Assembly type
Teacher-led assembly for all ages.

What you need
A backdrop display of pictures of Ayers Rock (Uluru) and of Australian Aboriginals, copy of photocopiable page 161.

What to do
Ask the children to shut their eyes, then adapt the assembly text on page 161 to your own style.

Prayer/reflection
Invite the children to listen or join with you:
In the beginning the world was made,
In the beginning was the dreamtime.

Think of a time when the mountains rose,
Think of a time when the rivers snaked their way across the land,
Think of a time when the pounding seas shaped the shores,
Think of a time when the great rock,
Uluru grew in the desert.

Blessed be the mountains,
Blessed be the rivers,
Blessed be the pounding seas,
And blessed be the sacred places,
Mosque, cathedral, temple and rock.

Further activity
Hold a general discussion about visiting a church or mosque. The children could do research to find out the ways of showing respect in these different places.

22. Stories of the land

Assembly type
Teacher-led assembly for all ages.

What you need
Optional: picture of Uluru (Ayers rock), copy of photocopiable page 162.

What to do
All cultures have stories of why things are as they are, including the presence of a natural phenomenon. Such stories give a sense of the place of landscape in our lives and how it affects us. The follow-up activity encourages the children to look more closely at their local area and think more imaginatively about it. The example chosen is the Australian Aboriginal tribe's story about Uluru, but a story from another tradition could be readily substituted. If the children have heard about Ayers Rock or Uluru before, remind them of it. If not, use the opening two paragraphs of the previous assembly. Then go on with the assembly text on page 162 in your own style.

Prayer/reflection
Read the prayer from the previous assembly (page 61) and ask the children to join in.

Further activities
• Discuss local landscape features with the children. The features need not be large ones; they could be a ditch running through a local park, or a hill, the shape of which is barely recognisable because it is covered in roads and housing, or a piece of barren land, or a gnarled old tree. Ask the children to choose one of these features and write a story about how it came to be. The ideas from the infants may be more quick and natural than the juniors, even though it appears at first to be a difficult task.
• Find other stories which explain landscape features, such as the Giant's Causeway in Northern Ireland.

CHAPTER 4

Science

This chapter looks at worship related to science topics. These assemblies are designed to help children to celebrate the natural world, to explore their own relationship with it and to think about their responsibilities for it. They are loosely linked with the programmes of study in the Science National Curriculum which cover Life Processes and Living Things, and Experimental and Investigative Science.

The assemblies in this chapter are rooted in a Christian understanding that the universe, and all within it, is a good place, although sometimes it can arouse fear or raise questions and problems. It is to be marvelled at and treasured and it has worth in its own right, not just as it relates to humanity. However, humanity has been given the privilege and the responsibility of imposing order on it, enjoying its fruits and taking care of it. This is a view which is, in essence, also shared by both Jews and Muslims, though the latter lay even greater stress on the idea that the world belongs to God and humanity acts as a caretaker for it. The Eastern faiths have some similar notions, but have a deeper sense of humanity being an integral part of the natural world, rather than something distinct from it. This is also a view held by many humanists, but without the theistic foundations which are the basis of the Christian beliefs.

The variety of life – animals

This series of assemblies looks at individual animals, suggesting ideas on how they many be celebrated in an assembly as well as how the ambiguity of reactions to them may be recognised. The question of humanity's responsibilities for animals is also raised. The assemblies serve, of course, as examples. There are many other assemblies on animals which could be planned on the same model. They are all best linked with class topic work.

1. A bird dance

Assembly type
A class assembly for top juniors built on a dance activity.

Stage 1 – Preparation

What you need
Card, scissors, felt-tipped pens, elastic, scrap materials, adhesive, stapler, copy of photocopiable page 163.

What to do
This assembly is dependent on the children having studied the local birdlife, by visiting a local park, observing a birdtable at school or reporting on birds seen in their own garden.

Read the assembly poem on page 163 to the children and talk about it with them. Don't worry about the fact that they will only understand the gist of the poem and not the detail of the imagery at the end. Ask them to talk about the birds visiting their gardens. Do they fly away like the bird in the poem?

Write and choreograph together a story of birds visiting the garden, bringing out in the dance the fact that the smaller birds are frightened of bigger ones. Help the children develop a movement which conveys the freedom of flight. The dance might include a cat visiting the garden and the birds' reaction to it.

Let the children make and decorate masks for their dance-drama.

Stage 2 – Assembly

What you need
Masks and dance story (see Preparation), tambourine.

What to do
Ask one child to introduce what the class has been studying, then introduce and read the assembly poem.

Let one group of children perform their dance of the garden visitors while the rest read the story. Use the tambourine to accent the dance and poem.

Prayer/reflection
We give thanks for the birds and other creatures that visit our gardens.
We want them to come.
We want them to have nothing to fear.

Let us be sure that we do them no harm.
We are glad that they can fly away when danger does come.

Song/hymn
Come and Praise
3 All things bright and beautiful
79 From the tiny ant

2. The elephant – an endangered species

Assembly type
An all-age teacher-led assembly for a class or the whole school.

What you need
Pictures of African elephants in native surroundings, a large sign that reads 'In Danger', pins or Blu-Tack, a map of the world, copy of photocopiable page 164.

What to do
Ask the children if they can guess which animal you are thinking of from the clue words 'large, grey, has a trunk'.

Tell them that there are two sorts of elephants, but that today you are going to talk about the ones that live in Africa. Then put up a picture

of the African elephant and stick the 'In Danger' sign across it. Explain that you might also have used the word 'dangerous', because the African elephant can be very dangerous. Continue, adapting the assembly text on page 164 to your own style.

Prayer/reflection
Listen to or say together the excerpt from the *Rime of the Ancient Mariner* (see page 17).

Song/hymn
Come and Praise
73 When your Father made the world
79 From the tiny ant

Further activity
Work with the children to make a display in the classroom or hall on one or more of the following themes:
• the work of an environmental charity or pressure group such as Greenpeace or WWF (see Resources, page 192);
• the situation of endangered species. Perhaps each class could 'adopt' an endangered species (for example whales or dolphins), informing the whole school, and thereafter providing updates and news items.

3. The spider

Assembly type
Classroom assembly for all ages.

What you need
Pencils, scrap paper, copy of photocopiable page 165.

What to do
Spiders hold a certain fascination, while often arousing unreasonable fear, even in a country with no dangerous spiders. Perhaps this common phobia occurs because of their quick movement. Spiders clearly demonstrate humanity's mixed feelings about the natural world.

Ask the children to write down anything which comes into their heads when you say the word, 'spider', while you count to thirty. Then ask the children to read out their reactions. There will probably be a fair amount of ambivalence expressed in the reactions. Comment on this and also comment on the use of the word 'big' if they have chosen it. After all, spiders are small in relation to humans.

Remind the children of the nursery rhyme 'Little Miss Muffet' which conveys the common idea that spiders are frightening. Ask for their opinions on where that fear comes from. Then read them the assembly story on page 165 which tells a famous legend about a spider.

Comment then on how some people reach for a duster when they see a cobweb. Others think it is something beautiful. Some people shove spiders out of their homes as fast as possible or even kill them. Others welcome them into the home as another small creature to share it.

Prayer/reflection
Ask the children if they want to add any new things to their lists about spiders. Then, using the words they have suggested but trying to evoke a variety of emotions, let them compose a simple poetic description beginning and ending with the words 'The spider'.

Song/hymn
Sing 'Incy-wincy spider' with the children. Comment on the persistence of the spider in the rhyme – it always begins to climb again as soon as the sun comes out.

Further activities
• Ask the children to look out for spiders' webs and make detailed pencil drawings of them. With younger children, make pictures with silver glitter on black paper of dew bejewelled webs.
• Encourage the children to do further research into spiders.
• Read one of the West Indian Anansi tales. These are about a spiderman and depict traditional Afro-Caribbean images of spiders.

Cats

These four sessions for infants encourage the children to think about cats' needs, take delight in them, and explore and acknowledge their own feelings about cats (not all of the children will like them, of course). These assemblies could be used as a series but this is not essential.

4. An imaginary class cat

Assembly type
An activity lasting over the whole of the day, ending with a short assembly, which could be done with nursery children as well as infants. It would be best to make it into an integrated day on 'Cats'.

What you need
A book about caring for cats, a cat basket, paint, brushes, paper, crayons, some quiet peaceful music.

What to do
Tell the children that you thought that it would be nice to have a class kitten but that there would be all sorts of problems with having a real one, so for the day you will have an imaginary one. Pretend to take the cat out of the basket and, while 'playing' with it on your knee, ask the children how you will need to look after it. Particularly question any cat owners for their advice and experience. Put 'the kitten' back in the basket while you read with the children a simple reference book on looking after cats. Conduct a quick ballot to name the cat.

As one of the day's activities, ask the children to paint a picture of what they think the cat looks like. As the day passes, make comments on where the cat is and what it is doing.

At the end of the day, have the children sit in a circle and together look at their paintings. Then pretend to take the kitten out of the basket, and hold it as though it were wriggling before passing it from one child to the next. When it 'returns' to you, pretend to stroke it and put it carefully back in the basket. Tell the children to speak very softly so that the kitten can sleep.

Ask the children what they felt like when they were holding the kitten. Were they

worried about anything? Encourage the children to talk about their own reactions to cats, including the fact that one or two children may be allergic to them.

Play some soft music and ask the children to stroke a pretend cat in time to it.

Prayer/reflection

Ask the children to name any cats they know well, not necessarily their own pets, and invite them to repeat after you: We hope that all cats everywhere and especially [cat's name] will be warm, well fed and loved.

Song/hymn

Come and Praise
19 He's got the whole world (adjust the words to include a reference to the kitten)
79 From the tiny ant
80 All the animals

5. Cats sleep anywhere

Assembly type

A whole school assembly with contributions from a class of infants. If the poem were omitted, it could also be done with nursery children.

Stage 1 – Preparation

What you need

The poem 'Cats' by Eleanor Farjeon (in *I like this poem* edited by Kaye Webb), *My Cat Likes to Hide in Boxes* by Eve Sutton and Lynley Dodd, large sheet of paper, felt-tipped pens.

What to do

Read the book and the poem to the class. Ask the children about their own cats and where they sleep or hide, making a list of the different places the children say on a large sheet of paper; for example, Emma's cat sleeps in the laundry basket.

Use the book as the basis for a simple mimed play. Rehearse the children reading the poem and doing the mime.

Stage 2 – Assembly

What you need
The poem 'Cats' by Eleanor Farjeon in *I like this poem*, TS Eliot's *Old Possum's Book of Practical Cats*, the list of statements about where cats sleep, the cat paintings from the previous assembly (4. An imaginary class cat).

What to do
Make a display of the pictures of the class's imaginary cats from the previous assembly and the list of cats' sleeping places.

Ask a small group of children to read the poem 'Cats', then let the others read out the statements about the sleeping habits of cats. Ask the children to perform the mime.

Read 'Jennyanydots' from *Old Possum's Book of Practical Cats*, introducing it by saying, 'We have heard about cats sleeping, but is that all they do? What do they do at night? The poet TS Eliot wondered about that and wrote a poem about it. This is the poem...'

Prayer/reflection
Ask the children to close their eyes and imagine they are a cat contentedly asleep somewhere.

Song/hymn
Come and Praise
80 All the animals

Further activity
Ask the children to write about the real habits of cats they know and what they imagine they might do at night.

6. The problem with cats

Assembly type
Classroom assembly for nursery, infant and lower junior children.

What you need
Pictures of garden birds and animals.

What to do
Although designed for infant children, this issue could be raised with older children. With the children, brainstorm the names of animals, including birds, who live in or visit their yards or gardens. If they have little experience of this, tell the children about creatures which have visited your home and show them pictures of such birds and animals. Invite the children to come out in turn and pretend

to be one of the garden visitors. Ask them to imagine what the attitude of these animals and birds would be to a cat coming to live in a house and why they would think that way.

Go on to talk about the problem of cats destroying small wildlife. Try to bring out the ambivalence many owners feel about their cats, especially when dead birds are brought in. Discuss the fact that cats have a natural instinct to hunt and that death is part of life.

Prayer/reflection
Let's think about cats and all the pleasure they bring. Let's also be sad about the animals they sometimes kill.

7. The death of a cat

Assembly type
A classroom assembly for top infants and lower juniors.

What you need
Fred by Posy Simmonds or *The Christmas Day Kitten* by James Herriot.

What to do
The death of a pet is something that many children experience and an inevitability with which they have to live. At the younger end of the age range, the children may not be fully aware of the permanence of death. This is something that they may be just coming to at the infant stage. Don't be surprised, either, if some of the children have a morbid approach to death, delighting in all the gory details. This is also quite common at this stage. Obviously, it is a subject which must be handled with sensitivity, but it is important that children learn to articulate their memories and griefs as this is a vital part of learning to mourn and handle bereavement.

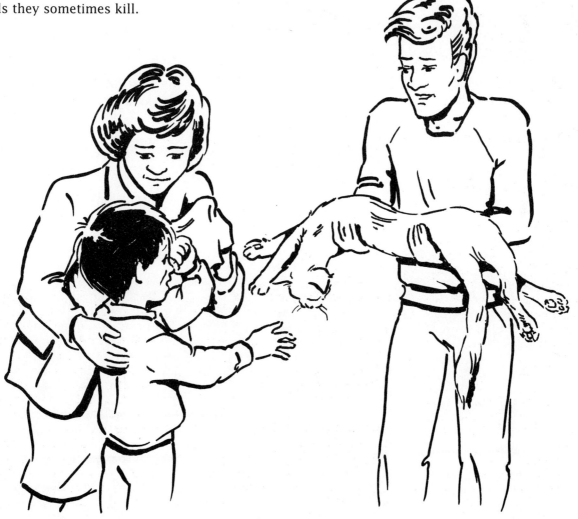

Fred is a book which combines humour with pathos. It brings out the ambivalence of cat ownership, the contrast between a cat's day and night life in a similar way to the Eliot poem, and also the need for ritual and mourning at the time of bereavement. *The Christmas Day Kitten* tackles the issue in a very different and perhaps more moving way, but without the counterbalancing humour.

Read one of the books and then invite the children to make general comment and to talk about a pet that has died and how they remember it.

Prayer/reflection
Let's sit quietly and give thanks for the lives of pets who have died or run away.

Further activity
Ask the children to draw a scene from the story or to draw and write about a pet which has died.

Snakes

Snakes and snake imagery have often had a central place in world religious practice, perhaps because of the power of snakes to mesmerise and bewitch. This power is expressed in the content of all three assemblies on the theme.

The opportunity to see and handle live snakes would greatly enhance these assemblies. If possible, invite into school a local herpetologist, perhaps a parent or friend, to introduce the children to a snake collection. The children will probably be surprised to discover that snakes are neither slimy nor cold.

8. Adam and Eve

Assembly type
Teacher-led assembly for children aged seven and upwards.

What you need
Pictures of snakes (optional), copy of photocopiable page 166.

What to do
This story, found in Genesis 3, is a core story in the Christian and Jewish faiths, and is one which continues to have a major influence on Western culture. It is important then for the children to become familiar with the story and to have some understanding of how Christians have interpreted it. In this version, the focus is on humanity's relationship to the snake, although it has, of course, many other powerful themes including freedom, alienation from nature, and why there is death. (The story of Adam and Eve's disobedience also appears in the Qur'an, but there is no mention of a snake.)

Adapt the assembly story on page 166 to your own style.

Go on to explain that in the Middle East, where this story was first told, and in many other parts of the world, this is indeed what happens. Snakes slither through the grass and bite people on the heel and people kill snakes by stamping on their heads.

Talk about different attitudes to the story, explaining how some Christians and Jews think that this is what actually happened about six thousand years ago. Other Christians and Jews do not believe it was a historical event but think that the story is talking about how people behave now: how they disobey God, how men and women treat each other, as well as the fear that lots of people have of snakes.

Prayer/reflection
Think quietly about the story and those ideas.

9. The Yanomamo

Assembly type
Teacher-led assembly for juniors.

What you need
Tape of South American music or the musical *Yanomamo* by Peter Rose and Anne Conlon (available from WWF, see Resources, page 192), pictures of jungle and anacondas (optional), copy of photocopiable page 167.

What to do
Remind the children of the role of the snake in the Biblical story of the expulsion of the first man and woman from the garden, and how the first woman had stopped and listened to the snake and so had been tempted to eat the fruit. Perhaps she had been mesmerised by the snake. Perhaps it had stared at her so she couldn't run away; it is said that some snakes terrify their prey with their stare before they strike. The story in the Bible also calls the snake the most subtle or devious of all creatures.

Continue with the assembly text on page 167 or adapt it to your own style.

Prayer/reflection
In the beginning,
say the Yanomamo,
In the beginning
they learnt from the giant anaconda snake.

They learnt from him to live in the jungle,
taking only what they need,
treating it with care,
treating it with respect.
May we learn to treat our world with care.
May we learn to treat it with respect.

Music
South American music or an excerpt from the musical *Yanomamo*.

Further activities
• Ask the children to paint pictures of the giant snake, trying to convey wisdom and terror at the same time.
• Encourage the class to find out about the animals of the Amazonian jungle and the work of conservation agencies in these areas.

• Learn the songs from *Yanomamo*.
• Read the zoo chapter from *Mary Poppins* by PL Travers which features an anaconda snake as wise and terrifying.

10. 'Snake' by DH Lawrence

Assembly type
Teacher-led assembly for juniors, but you will need to practise reading the poem.

What you need
A copy of the poem 'Snake' by DH Lawrence (it is available in many modern anthologies or in *Complete Poems of DH Lawrence*).

What to do
This poem captures the sense of fear and fascination which is evoked by the snake and which has been explored in the last two assemblies. Remind the children of the two previous assemblies and the ancient stories about the snake. Tell them that the poem is fairly modern. Ask them to listen for how the poet feels about the snake, then read the poem.

Prayer/reflection
Ask the children to close their eyes and imagine they were watching a snake, as fascinated as Lawrence was.

Further activities
• Discuss with the children Lawrence's feelings about and response to the snake.
• Ask the children to write about a real or imaginary encounter with an animal during which they were fascinated and scared at the same time.

The family of creation

The nature of our relationship with animals and with the natural world in general is the topic of much discussion. These assemblies begin to explore some aspects of this debate.

11. Learning from animals

Assembly type
Short assembly for a class or larger group of all ages.

What you need
Pictures of a cat, a grasshopper, a stork, and an ant, copy of photocopiable page 168.

What to do
The attribution of human qualities to animals is commonplace. It forms the basis for many similes and is often used in stories to draw a moral, as in Aesop's fables. The following is adapted from the Jewish book, the Talmud, which is a commentary of story and discussion on the Jewish scriptures.

Before the assembly, make a display of the animal pictures. Adapt the assembly text on page 168 to your own style.

Prayer/reflection
Think about an animal you know and like, perhaps a dog or a cat or a bird that visits your yard or garden. Think about something you wish people could learn from this animal.

Song/hymn
Come and Praise
80 All the animals

Music
Saint-Saëns *Carnival of the Animals*

Further activities
• Discuss with the children whether or not they think people can learn from animals

and also the contrast between the sentiment of the assembly and the accusation, 'You are behaving like animals'.
• Ask the children to think of other popular similes involving animals. Are they all positive? Read the children one or more of Aesop's fables.
• Ask the children to devise a dance to the music of *Carnival of the Animals* depicting the variety of animal life.

12. Caring for animals

Assembly type
All-age assembly.

What you need
Copy of photocopiable page 169.

What to do
This story is taken from the Hadith, the collection of traditions about the prophet

Muhammad. Muslims have a great respect for Muhammad, so after his death they collected together people's memories of what he had done and said during his life. They try to learn from his example.

Introduce the story by saying that Muslims have a number of stories about their prophet Muhammad and his attitude to animals. These stories show Muslims how they should treat animals, and non-Muslims can learn from them too. Adapt the assembly text on page 169 to your own style.

Prayer/reflection
May we always pay attention and be observant so that we don't hurt other creatures.

Song/hymn
Come and Praise
79 From the tiny ant
80 All the animals

Further activity
Organise a discussion about not hurting animals. This might include the issue of vegetarianism.

13. Who is my family?

Assembly type
Teacher-led assembly for the class or whole school, all ages.

What you need
A picture of St Francis, preferably showing him speaking to the wolf (optional), copy of photocopiable page 170.

What to do
Ask the children to put their hands up if they have sisters or brothers, and ask them to name other relationships in the family, such as mother, father and cousins. Perhaps bring one or two of the family groups to the front. Comment on how brothers and sisters don't always get on but how there is often a great bond between them. Adapt the assembly story on page 170 to your own style.

Francis wrote a song about the different creatures that God made. Some people call it 'The Canticle of the Sun', but a better name for it is 'The Canticle of the Creatures'.

Prayer
Listen to some of the Canticle of the Creatures:

Be praised then, my Lord God,
In and through your creatures,
Especially among them,
Through our noble Brother Sun,
By whom you light our day;
In his radiant splendid beauty
He reminds us, Lord, of you....

In Brother Wind be praised, my Lord,
And in the air
In cloud, in calm,
In all the weather moods that cherish life....

Through our dear Mother Earth be praised, my Lord,
She feeds us, guides us, gives us plants, bright flowers,
And all her fruits.

(From the translation by Molly Reidy. A full translation appears in the *Assisi Declarations*, available from WWF – see Resources, page 192.)

Song/hymn
Come and Praise
7 All creatures of our God and King
78 The song of St Francis (By brother sun)
(both these are adaptations of the Canticle of the Creatures.)

Further activities
• Find out more about St Francis.
• Discuss further the symbol of the family.

Trees

The tree is a key symbol of life. According to the Bible, the tree of life stood in the garden of Eden as well as the tree of the knowledge of good and evil, and it is said to stand in Paradise. These assemblies are designed to encourage children to value trees as intrinsic to life, and to show the children that they have a role to play in caring for them.

14. Caring for trees

Assembly type
Assembly for all ages, either as the first of a series or on its own.

What you need
Pictures of fruit trees, display materials, copy of photocopiable page 171.

What you do
Before the assembly, prepare a display of pictures of fruit trees. Ask the children to close their eyes and listen carefully to what you are saying. Adapt the assembly text on page 171 to your own style.

Prayer/reflection
Imagine that you are back in that garden, but this time you are working to look after it.

Song/hymn
Come and Praise
16 When God made the garden of creation
73 When your Father made the world

Further activities
• Help the children to find out how trees are cared for, perhaps making a poster with words of advice about different trees.
• Discuss with the children ways of caring for any trees in the school grounds.
• Bring in different fruits and hold a fruit-tasting session with the children. Be aware of the possibility of children with food allergies relating to fruit.

15. The Bishnoi

Assembly type
Teacher-led assembly, either part of a series or on its own, for upper infants upwards.

What you need
Map of the world, pictures of desert places, display materials, copy of photocopiable page 172.

What to do
Before the assembly, make a display comprising a map of the world surrounded by pictures of desert places.

Remind the children of the first assembly on trees and tell them that today they will be hearing about a group of people known for their love of trees.

Adapt the assembly text on page 172 to your own style.

Prayer/reflection
In silence, think about the story.

Song/hymn
'Trees' by Eric Maddern (reproduced in the *REAL Scheme: Infant Assembly Book).
Come and Praise*
17 Think of a world without any flowers

Further activities
• Ask the children to do a report on their own neighbourhood from the point of view of a Bishnoi or a tree lover.

• Read to the children *The People Who Hugged Trees* adapted by Deborah Lee Rose. This is about the Chipko people whose story is similar to that of the Bishnoi.

• Help the children to find out why trees are so important to the environment. Older children could investigate the effects of deforestation.

• Help the children compare historical and modern maps of Britain or their local area, to see how much deforestation has taken place in this country. Place names can sometimes give clues; for example, the New Forest has very little forest area now.

• Ask children to find out about products from trees.

• Older children could make a comparative study of the amount of time it takes different trees to grow, finding out which can be renewed quickly and therefore farmed.

16. Trees – a story from the Islamic faith

Assembly type
Teacher-led assembly for all ages, either as part of a series or on its own.

What you need
Some dates, and a picture of a date tree, copy of photocopiable page 173.

What to do
This story is adapted from the Hadith, a collection of sayings of Muhammad and stories about his life (see assembly on 'Caring for animals', page 75).

Show the children the dates and invite one or two to taste them. Explain that dates grow at the top of very tall trees, and show them the picture of the date palm. Then tell the assembly story on page 173, explaining that it comes from the Islamic faith.

Prayer/reflection
May we grow in wisdom, learning to enjoy the fruits of trees without damaging them.

Song/hymn
Come and Praise
6 The earth is yours, O God
11 For the beauty of the earth
16 When God made the garden of creation
73 When your Father made the world

Further activity
Discuss with the children ways that trees can be damaged by children, sometimes accidentally and sometimes on purpose.

17. Adopt a tree

Assembly type
Classroom activity for infants followed by a classroom reflection.

Stage 1 – Preparation

What you need
Pencils, paper, boards, art paper, paint, crayons.

What to do
Identify nearby a deciduous tree which has enough space in front of it for the children to sit and draw comfortably. Let the children visit the tree at

least four times over the course of a year. This will not only give the children a scientific objective knowledge of the tree, and develop observational skills, but will also lead to an affection for the tree and help nurture a positive attitude to trees. It is a particularly valuable activity for inner-city children who may have so few trees in the locality that they go virtually unnoticed.

On each visit to the tree, ask the children to sketch it. Follow this up with work in the classroom which should include:
• painting or crayoning a picture of the tree using the sketch as a guide;
• a scientific observational report;
• a short poem trying to capture how they felt about the tree in its current state or using images to describe it. An acrostic poem on the word 'tree' could be used to get them started.

Stage 2 – Assembly

What to do
Look at some of the children's tree paintings, then read the tree poems.

Prayer/reflection
Let us close our eyes and imagine our tree and give thanks for its beauty.

Song/hymn
'Trees' by Eric Maddern (printed in *REAL Scheme: Infant Assembly Book*).
Come and Praise
3 All things bright and beautiful
5 Somebody greater

18. Our tree

Assembly type
Class assembly for the whole school, based on the previous activity.

Stage 1 – Preparation

What you need
Children's work from the previous assembly, percussion instruments.

What to do
Look back with the children at the story of the tree through the year, and recollect how it has changed. Choose a sample

of the artwork and a piece of poetry from each season and sequence them to tell the story. Help the children make up a simple percussion rhythm or tune to go between each reading and ask one child to write an introduction.
Learn a tree song to sing together.

Stage 2 - Assembly

What you need
Chosen tree poems and a display of the chosen accompanying art work (see Preparation), percussion instruments.

What to do
Tell the story of the tree throughout the year. Let one child introduce the tree. Then

for each season of the year, have one child read a poem, followed by others playing the percussion tune for that season.

Song/hymn
Come and Praise
3 All things bright and beautiful
5 Somebody greater

The sun and the moon

19. The sun

Assembly type
An assembly requiring classroom preparation at junior level, but which could be given to the whole primary range.

Stage 1 - Preparation

What you need
Paper, pens, paint, newspaper, paste, percussion instruments.

What to do
This assembly helps the children to think about their relationship to a natural phenomenon.

After a science session about the sun have a brainstorming session, trying to draw out from the children that the sun is necessary for both life and growth. It is the source of both heat and light on earth. Trace back various forms of power and light to see how they originally stored energy from the sun. For example, electricity can be made from wind generators, air currents make wind, and sunlight heats the air to make air currents. The sun is also something to be feared and respected because of its power to burn. Draw the material together, either as a class or with the children working individually or in small groups, to write a poem praising the qualities of the sun but also expressing its power. Encourage the children to compose a percussion accompaniment to enhance it further.

Ask the children either to paint an enormous picture of the sun or to make a papier mâché model.

Stage 2 – Assembly

What you need
A Bible, the sun poem, the sun picture or model (see Preparation), the words of Psalm 104:1-6 on a poster or overhead projector transparency, copy of photocopiable page 174.

What to do
Put the picture or model as a focal point for the assembly.

Start with the children saying or chanting their poem about the sun. Then tell them that in many parts of the ancient world people used to worship the sun as a god because they recognised how important it was in their lives. Then adapt the assembly text on page 174 to your own style.

Ask a child to read Psalm 104:1-6.

Prayer/reflection
Invite the rest of the children to read the psalm with you.

Song/hymn
Come and Praise
1 Morning has broken
7 All creatures of our God and King
11 For the beauty of the earth
12 Who put the colours in the rainbow?
78 Song of St Francis (By brother sun)

20. Is seeing believing?

Assembly type
A whole-school assembly, requiring some preparation by a class beforehand.

Stage 1 – Preparation

What you need
Paper to record observations, pens, cardboard, paint, scissors, a torch, a balloon or a ball.

What to do
This assembly might follow on from the previous one or it can stand on its own in a topic on the earth in space. The scientific material is covered in Key Stage 1 in the National Curriculum.

During the course of the day, observe the position of the sun in the sky relative to a marker in the playground such as a tree, a goal post or a climbing frame, recording the result on a diagram. At the end

of the day look at the results. Discuss with the children why people talk about the sun rising and setting, and how in the past people thought the sun went round the earth. Demonstrate how the earth goes round the sun by asking a child to shine a torch on a balloon which is being rotated by another child.

In another session, revise the previous work, then tell the children that the Ancient Greeks thought that every day the sun god drove his fiery chariot across the sky. Organise the children into groups to present their observations and what they have learned for the assembly. Prepare simple horse masks and a cardboard box chariot.

Stage 2 – Assembly

What you need
Pictures of Copernicus and Galileo, horse masks and chariot (see Preparation), torch, balloon, copy of photocopiable page 175.

What to do
Before the assembly, display the pictures of Galileo and Copernicus. Let one child introduce the study of the position of the sun in the sky, then let a group of children report on how the sun appeared to move across the sky over the playground.

Ask another child to give the Ancient Greek understanding, and organise a group of children dressed as horses with the chariot to gallop across the hall. Follow this by getting a third group of children to model the modern understanding of the reason for night and day, using a torch and a balloon.

Adapt the assembly text on page 175 to your own style.

Prayer/reflection
Invite the children to think quietly for a short time about being ready to listen and hear new ideas and different ways of viewing things.

Song/hymn
Come and Praise
42 Travel on
47 One more step

Further activities
• Let children in other classes do their own observations and look at the model again.
• Ask older children to find out more about Copernicus and Galileo.

21. The moon as a measure of time

Assembly type
Class or whole-school assembly preceded by classroom activity.

Stage 1 – Preparation

What you need
Copies of photocopiable page 176, pencils.

What to do
Distribute copies of photocopiable page 176 and ask the children to take the chart home and every night for a month fill in the shape of the moon that they observe. At the end of the month, identify when the new moon appeared and when it was the full moon. Help the children to see that the calendar month and the lunar month do not coincide.

Stage 2 – Assembly

What you need
A copy of photocopiable page 176 that has been filled in (see Preparation), a Bible, copy of photocopiable page 177.

What to do
This assembly is designed to help children think about their relationship to the natural world. Many festivals in different cultures are timed according to the phases of the moon. The Bible relates that the two lights of heaven were created to indicate festivals, days and years. Ask one of the children to read from Genesis 1:16.

Draw attention to a chart from photocopiable page 176, and make a general description of the moon changing from a thin sliver to full moon and back again. Tell the children that the new moon is often seen as something magical and mysterious, and adapt the assembly text on page 177 to your own style.

Prayer/reflection
Close your eyes and think quietly about that question.

Further activity
Ask the children to suggest other ways of telling the time from nature, then ask them to make a collage picture of these different ways.

22. The mystery of the moon

Assembly type
A junior class assembly with some classroom preparation which could be linked to a visit to a science museum.

Stage 1 – Preparation

What you need
Large picture of the full moon.

What to do
On the day of a fairly full moon, tell the children that in times past people would look up at the moon and the shadows on its surface and think to themselves that people or animals lived up there. Today we know that the shadows on the moon are caused by craters, but it is still fun to imagine what animals or people might live up there. Show the children the picture of the full moon and ask them of what the shadows remind them.

Remind them to try to look at the full moon when they go home that evening.

Stage 2 – Assembly

What you need
Copy of photocopiable page 178 (enlarged), picture of the full moon, copy of photocopiable page 179.

What to do
Remind the children of the shapes they saw in the moon, then tell them how the Ancient Chinese looked at the moon and saw a rabbit, a tree and a beautiful maiden on its surface. Show them the enlarged copy of photocopiable page 178.

The assembly story on page 179 tells how the maiden got there.

Further activities
• Ask the children to paint pictures of the shadows on the moon, making them look like animals or people.
• Let the children make paper lanterns in the shapes of fish or birds.

23. The Apollo expedition

Assembly type
A junior assembly with a classroom activity.

Stage 1 – Preparation

What you need
Books about the Apollo voyages, or resources from a visit to a science museum, paper, pencils.

What to do
Tell the children that they are going to put on a short play in assembly about the first landing on the moon, but they will have to do some research first. Ask them to find out as much as they can about the first landing in July 1969. Ask them to interview older friends and relatives to find out whether they watched the first landing on television and what their reactions were.

Alternatively or as well, ask older members of staff to come in and share their memories of the day. If you can find people who were in different parts of the world at the time it will help develop an understanding of different time zones.

Divide the children into groups to use the research to develop a short play. One group will be the astronauts, including the one still in the spacecraft, another group will be the technicians back at mission control, and the rest will be television reporters interviewing people to find out their reactions to the event.

Stage 2 – Assembly

What you need
Dressing-up clothes, a recording of Debussy's *Clair de Lune*, paper lanterns, torches, simple 'space helmets', (made from riding hats or bicycle crash helmets), copy of photocopiable page 180.

What to do
Tell the children that you are going to play some music

about the moonlight and ask them to imagine a field or a town in the moonlight while you play a part of *Clair de Lune.* Then adapt the assembly text on page 180 to your own style.

Prayer/reflection

Listen to what the Bible says about the moon.

> ...she waxes wonderfully in
> her phases,
> banner of the hosts on high,
> shining in the vault of
> heaven.

Ecclesiasticus 43:8-9, Jerusalem Bible, this book is not found in the Protestant Bible.
Listen again to *Clair de Lune.*

Further activities

• Write poems about the moon; perhaps haiku, poems in the shape of a new moon, or acrostics.
• Use *Clair de Lune* in dance lessons to create a dance of the moonlight.

Celebration of human difference

Children should know that individuals vary from one human to the next, and should be able to measure simple differences between each other. Too often, in the name of seeking a common bond, teachers pretend that there are no differences. This can leave the child who believes he is different from the norm feeling that he is an outsider, rather than accepting that each person is an individual and that there is no norm. In the Christian faith as it is expressed in the gospels, God knows each of us as distinct individuals, down to counting the hairs on our heads.

24. Fingerprints

Assembly type

Nursery or infant activity followed by reflection.

What you need

Paper, fairly thin paint in a bowl.

What to do

Take the thumbprints of everyone in the class on one large sheet of paper which you then display. Encourage the children to look closely to see if there are any two the same.

Comment on how amazing it is that with all the people there are in the world, no two people have exactly the same fingerprints. Encourage the children to feel a sense of wonder about it.

25. Being me

Assembly type
Infant activity followed by reflection.

What you need
Paper, pencils.

What to do
Ask the children to think about how people tell them apart from their friends and ask them to list as many contrasts as they can between themselves and their friends, for example, 'He has brown eyes, I have green,' or 'My hands are bigger than hers.' In some instances the children will find this absurd. In others they will have experienced adults getting muddled and confusing them with someone else.

Ask the children to read out their comparisons and see whether others can recognise their partners. Talk about identical twins and how there are some differences even if they can be difficult to see.

Prayer/reflection
Invite the children to clap for the fact that we all look different and this helps people recognise us.

26. Different people

Assembly type
Infant teacher-led assembly.

What you need
The book *People* by Peter Spier.

What to do
People by Peter Spier develops extensively the theme of difference, and the richness this brings the world. It is so rich that a whole series of conversations and assemblies could be built around it. You could also use *The Same but Different* by Tessa Dahl.

Select a few pages of the book to read and encourage the children to comment and talk about the examples of difference.

27. Masks

Assembly type
Infant class assembly to the whole school, preceded by classroom activity.

Stage 1 – Preparation

What you need
Copies of photocopiable page 181, paper, felt-tipped pen, scissors, card, adhesive.

What to do

Distribute copies of photocopiable page 181, then let the children paint the masks in identical colours and stick them on cardboard when they are dry. (Flattened cereal packets are a cheap source of cardboard.)

Write a class poem about 'Ways we are different'.

Stage 2 – Assembly

What you need

Masks (see Preparation).

What to do

Ask the children to wear their masks and parade before the school.

Ask the other children to try to pick out any they can recognise. If they manage it, despite the disguises, ask what gave them the clues. Afterwards make the point of how useful it is that people are all different.

Ask a group of children to read out the class poem.

Prayer/reflection

Let's give a cheer for difference. (*Cheer*).

28. The rhythm of the day

Assembly type

Infant writing or drawing activity followed by a dance reflection.

What you need

Paper, pencils, simple percussion instruments.

What to do

Ask the children to think of three things they do every day, then let them either write or draw about them.

Take several pieces of the children's writing and use them to form the story line of a simple repetitive mime dance. For example, every day I eat breakfast, I brush my teeth, I play football. Repeat the words several times, and use the percussion instruments to add to the sense of rhythm. Taking several examples will get away from the idea that there is a normal rhythm that every child follows. Whatever they have in common, overall the children's daily rhythms will be different.

Ask them to think whether something happens in the sky every day and then ask them to mime the activity of the sun and the moon. Use percussion instruments to evoke the sense of the sun rising and setting. Repeat the mime several times over to give a sense of rhythm.

Prayer/reflection

Ask the children to lie still and quiet, because every day every person must sleep.

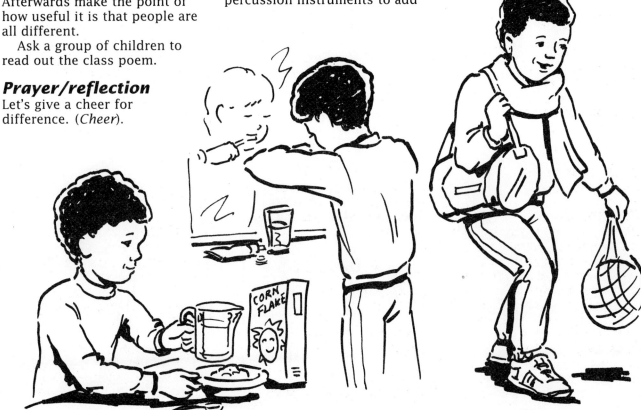

29. The rhythm of the year

Assembly type
Classroom assembly for infants.

What you need
A copy of *Anno's Counting Book*, Mitsumasa Anno.

What to do
Read *Anno's Counting Book* together. The pictures which follow the seasonal changes over an expanding village speak for themselves and are quite magical. The children will enjoy the counting and also predicting what will happen on the following page. The last page is often greeted by hushed silence from children viewing it for the first time.

Song/hymn
Come and Praise
110 Sing, people, sing
111 Round, round, round

30. The life cycle – babies

Assembly type
Class assembly for infants.

What you need
Pictures of babies.

What to do
Seat the children in a circle. Show them pictures of babies, then ask the children to imagine that there is a cradle in front of them with a baby in it. Tell them that the baby has begun to cry so they will need to pick it up and comfort it, picking up your own 'baby' at the same time. Guide the children through the fantasy of holding the baby – putting it over their shoulders very carefully and stroking its back and hair, returning it to a

rocking position and looking into its eyes and wondering what it is thinking, rocking it gently. Invite them to sing with you a lullaby or other song they know to help it sleep. Then ask them to lay it tenderly back in the cradle and tuck it in.

Talk to them quietly about mothers, fathers, grandparents and elder brothers and sisters all over the world, putting babies down to sleep, some in ornate expensive cots, and some in makeshift cradles. Tell the children how often the grown-up will watch over the baby as it is sleeping. They might feel happy that the baby is at last sleeping because it

has been crying for a long time. They often look and think how beautiful the baby is and wonder what will happen to it in the future. Then read the children the following poem, telling them it was written by a poor mother in India who felt worried about the future.

Down in a slum a new-born babe
Stirs in her sleep.
She wakes, she looks.
She looks into my eyes.
She looks into my eyes.
And I know we have hope.
I know we have hope.
(*Liturgy of life*)

Hymn/song
Sing another quiet song or lullaby.

31. The life cycle – children

Assembly type
Class assembly for infants.

What you need
Poem 'Now we are six' from the anthology of the same name by AA Milne, *Titch* by Pat Hutchins.

What to do
The poem 'Now we are six' by AA Milne expresses a deep sense of satisfaction at having become a person in one's own right.

Read the poem to the children at least twice, inviting them to comment on it. If the children are five or less, ask them what they are looking forward to about being six; if they are six, what they like about being six; and if they are seven or over what they liked about being six and what they like about their present age.

Then read them *Titch*. Ask them to comment on Titch's feelings at several stages in the story. What mixed feelings did he have about being a child of that size? What disadvantages do the children see for themselves? What things do they like about being their age?

Then invite the children to join in saying the poem with you.

32. The life cycle – adults

Assembly type
Class assembly for infants.

What you need
Paper, pencils.

What to do
The day before the assembly, ask the children to find out at least one thing that their parents or carers were doing while they were at school that day.

Seat the children in a circle and tell them that today they will be thinking about adults and the things they do while children are in school. Play a miming game, encouraging the children to act out something their parent or carer did the previous day so that the others can guess what it is. Ask two children to record the different activities (without worrying about spelling accuracy).

After each performance, applaud each child. If the activity has been something which has involved caring for the child's needs (for example, shopping, cooking, ironing or driving to collect the children from school), invite the children to give a second round of applause for the specific act of caring. However, make a point of also giving a positive comment on those activities which were not related to the child's needs.

33. For good or bad?

Assembly type
All age assembly, with a small amount of class preparation.

What you need
Pictures of wildlife, display materials, copy of photocopiable pages 182 and 183.

What to do
Before the assembly, choose and prepare either individual children or a chorus of readers to present the lament. Prepare a display of pictures of wildlife.

Begin by describing the fact that at that very moment scientists throughout the world are busy investigating chemicals and trying to solve problems facing humanity, and that today you will be telling the children about a powerful chemical combination discovered in 1939.

Then adapt the assembly text on pages 182 and 183 to your own style.

Prayer/reflection
Listen to these words:

And I, the Earth the Lord created
Cry aloud to my Maker,
Save me from ravage and destruction
To praise and glorify your name forever.

Mountains and hills, plants and trees,
Rivers and oceans, whales and fishes,
Birds, beasts and cattle,
Cry aloud to the Lord
Save us from destruction
To praise and magnify you forever
Save us! Save us! Save us!

(from the 'Benedicite lament' from the *Coventry Cathedral Creation Festival Liturgy,* WWF.)

Song/hymn
Come and Praise
11 For the beauty of the earth
14 All the nations of the earth

Further activities
• Ask the children to write a story about someone who did something out of good intentions which went all wrong.
• Help the children to research to identify other things which have their good uses but can also harm the environment (for example cars or plastics).
• Ask the children to paint a mural illustrating the lament.

CHAPTER 5

Maths

Maths can provide the inspiration for worship in several ways. Firstly, it may be a source of wonder when children are given the opportunities to consider the intricate patterns of nature, be bemused by scale and reflect on large numbers with infinity beyond them. Secondly, maths may raise issues of value, whether in the terms of the market exchange or in the way persons are named and counted. Thirdly, central religious ideas are expressed in mathematical form. Christians speak of God as three in one, and many faiths speak of the oneness of creation. These assemblies are linked to maths topics rather than specific attainment targets.

1. Too many to count

Assembly type
Infant school assembly.

What you need
Clipboard, pencil.

What to do
Brief a child or another adult to take on the role of someone from the 'Ministry of Numbers'. Prepare in advance a list of questions which move from the possible to the impossible (for example, how many windows are there in the room? How many teachers? How many people who own cats? How many freckles? How many bricks in the wall? How many hairs on someone's head? How many blades of grass in the local park? How many grains of sand on a beach? How many stars in the sky?). Start by talking on any subject and then arrange to be interrupted by the other adult or child coming into the room and announcing officiously that he is from the Ministry of Numbers and he wants to know the answer to certain questions. As he reads out each question, involve the children as you try to answer the questions. The official should meanwhile be filling in the list. Comment at the end that some of the numbers were too big even to think about, let alone count!

Prayer/reflection
Listen to Psalm 33:6-7, 13-16, 20-22 and/or Matthew 10:29-31.

Song/hymn
Come and Praise
15 God knows me

Further activity
Help the children as a class or in pairs to make up lists of things which are too numerous to count.

2. A counting story

Assembly type
School assembly for infants and older.

What you need
Ten sacks, a drum, copy of photocopiable page 184.

What to do
There are many versions of this story. This one is adapted from an Ethiopian tale.

Either rehearse children beforehand to perform the story as a play or choose ten children whom you will direct to act the story as you go along. As you describe the counting, act it out, counting with the children (but each time missing out the one who is counting), and get one child to beat the drum at the appropriate time.

Start by giving the children sacks which you tell them are full of grains of wheat which they are taking to the big town to be ground into flour. Explain that it is a hard journey to the town because they have to cross a vast plain where leopards live. Tell them that they are feeling nervous of the leopards. Then adapt the assembly story on page 184 to your own style.

Then ask the children to explain what happened, if they haven't already done so.

Prayer/reflection
Let us all remember that when we are thinking about other people, we count too.

Song/hymn
Come and Praise
15 God knows me
10 God who made the earth

3. The Good Shepherd

Assembly type
Infant school assembly.

What you need
A children's version of 'The Good Shepherd' (Luke 15:3-6) or your own adaptation.

What to do
Describe to the children the conditions of shepherding in Biblical times; how the sheep were counted into a simple enclosure each night and how the shepherd would light a fire and lie down at the gate and guard the sheep.

Tell the story, and involve the children in re-enacting the counting of the sheep into the fold as the shepherd finds he only has 99 sheep, repeating the exercise for dramatic effect though not necessarily counting all the way up to one hundred. Emphasise the fact that the shepherd cares for each one of his sheep individually, and rejoices when the last one is found. The missing one was important although there were 100 sheep.

Prayer/reflection
Read the opening verses of Psalm 23, explaining to children that the person who wrote it believed that God looked after him like a shepherd looking after his sheep.

Song/hymn
Come and Praise
19 He's got the whole world
10 God who made the earth
15 God knows me

4. The chess board

Assembly type
Junior school or class assembly.

What you need
A chess board, a bag of rice, copy of photocopiable page 185.

What to do
Tell the assembly story on page 185, showing the chess board and the rice at the appropriate moments. The

story is intended to evoke a feeling of wonder at the concept of number.

Prayer/reflection
Stop and think silently about how surprising and interesting numbers can be.

Further activity
Ask children who are able in maths to work out how many grains would go on each square as far as they possibly can. Present the findings on a poster drawn up as a chessboard.

5. A name not a number

Assembly type
Infant and junior school assembly.

What you need
Items with personal numbers on, such as a cheque book or bank card.

What to do
This assembly links in with the cross-curricular themes of economic understanding and citizenship. Tell the children about all the personal numbers you have and why you have them. These could include National Insurance, telephone, bank account, car registration and credit card numbers. Comment how the official who looks at your number probably never thinks of you as a person, but rather as just a number. Talk briefly too about prisoner of war camps where people were called by a number rather than a name.

Raise the question of why parents give their children names and not numbers. Could the children imagine being called Number 3 or Number 5 instead of by their names?

Comment again that calling people numbers is a way of stopping thinking of them as a real person. Numbers have their uses but not for everything.

Tell the children that in many faiths it is said that God knows each person by name. When a new baby is born, God doesn't think, 'That is number one billion, two thousand, and twenty-four' or something like that. He knows them as an individual person. He knows them by name.

Prayer/reflection
We each have a name, because we are each a unique person. Let us be proud of our names.

Listen to the words from the Bible in Isaiah 40:26 and Isaiah 43:1-3.

6. Patterns

Assembly type
A classroom assembly for all ages.

What you need
Some natural objects, such as an onion cut in half, a piece of celery, daisies, buttercups, leaves or shells, paper, pencils.

What to do
This activity should encourage the children to develop a sense of wonder at natural objects by looking at them more closely.

Display the various natural objects on the table and ask the children to sketch them individually and with great care. Assemble the children as a group, look at a selection of the sketches as well as the original objects and encourage the children to comment on any patterns they may have noticed (for example, spirals or rough symmetry).

Prayer/reflection
There are patterns in the world;
There are patterns in what we see;
There are patterns in what we hear;
There are patterns in what we do;
We celebrate the wonder of patterns.

Song/hymn
Come and Praise
11 For the beauty of the earth
12 Who put the colours in the rainbow?

7. Celtic knot patterns

Assembly type
Junior school assembly.

What you need
Copies of photocopiable page 186, felt-tipped pens, overhead projector, a piece of unfinished knitting, examples of weaving.

What to do
Before the assembly, prepare overhead projector transparencies by tracing

photocopiable page 186 using coloured felt-tipped pens.

Talk to the children about the problems encountered when knitting a jumper. For example, explain how you have to be careful that you don't drop a stitch, otherwise the whole thing will begin to unravel. Describe how knitting is a process of linking knots. Look at the examples of weaving and perhaps ask a child to describe the process.

Ask the children to look at the fabrics they are wearing and see how they are either linked or woven together to make a whole.

Using the overhead projector, show the children the Celtic knot patterns and explain that the Celts expressed in their patterns the idea that we were linked together almost like a big piece of knitting; that what one person does affects another, and that people and nature are all interconnected.

Draw on connections you know of in school. For example, Sarah and Matthew are in two different classes but Sarah is friends with Emily whose little brother is John whose friend is Carl whose big brother is Matthew.

Prayer/reflection
A traditional Celtic prayer:

God over me, God under me,
God before me, God behind me,
I on thy path, O God,
Thou, O God, in my steps.

(From *God in Our Midst* by Martin Reith.)

Further activities
• Using photocopiable page 186, make Celtic patterns available for the children to colour. Encourage them to experiment to draw a simple knot pattern themselves.
• Look at items of clothing and tinned fruit and vegetables, both of which have their country of origin on them. Help the children to see how there is a connection between themselves and people all over the world.

8. Islamic Patterns

Assembly type
Classroom preparation followed by junior school assembly.

Stage 1 – Preparation

What you need
Examples of different sorts of patterns, copies of photocopiable page 187, felt-tipped pens, paper, pencils.

What to do
This assembly is linked to History SSUA, Houses and places of worship, as well as maths, and aims to encourage children to think about the necessity or otherwise of rules and making rules which are consistent with one another. Before the assembly, distribute copies of photocopiable page 187, which show Islamic interlocking patterns. Encourage the children to discover the way the patterns repeat themselves. Put these patterns on display outside the assembly hall with invitations for the children to look at them closely.

Talk about making different sorts of patterns. Invite a child to come forward and ask her to make a scribble pattern, letting her pencil 'go for a walk' freely across the page. Let another child design his own repeating pattern. Draw out from him that having made the rules of the pattern in the initial box, he has to follow those rules to make the rest of the pattern work.

Stage 2 – Assembly

What you need
A selection of Islamic patterns (see Preparation), copy of photocopiable page 188.

What to do
Ask one or two of the children who have coloured in the Islamic patterns to talk about

anything they discovered, and to show the rest of the children a selection of the patterns.

Then adapt the assembly text on page 188 to your own style.

Prayer/reflection
Listen to these words from the Qur'an:

He created the heavens and the earth in true proportions: He makes the night overlap the day, and the day overlap the night: He has subjected the sun and moon to His law, each one follows a course for the time appointed.
Is He not the exalted power – He who forgives again and again?

(Sura 7:54)

Further activities
• Make more Islamic patterns available for the children to colour.

• Give the children one rule and ask them to think about patterns of behaviour which are consistent with it. For example, 'Be kind to others' implies that you don't fight and you don't humiliate others.

9. Scale

Assembly type
Infant and junior school assembly, based on a classroom activity.

Stage 1 – Preparation

What you need
Paper, pencils, one of the *Mrs Pepperpot* stories by Alf Prøysen.

What to do
Ask the children to think about how various objects would look to them if the children were the size of an ant or a mouse. What things would be easier to do? What things would be harder?

Read the children a *Mrs Pepperpot* story as an introduction, then ask them to write either a story beginning 'One morning I woke up and found I had shrunk to the size of a pepperpot' or a poem starting 'If I were a mouse, a... would be the size of a..., a... the size of a...' etc.

Then ask the children to think about being a giant. How would the world look to them? What problems and benefits would they have?

Stage 2 – Assembly

What you need
The children's poems and stories (see Preparation).

What to do
Ask the children to read their stories and poems to the school.

Prayer/reflection
Ask the children to shut their eyes and imagine how they would feel if they were very small, and then how they would feel if they were very large.

Further activities
• For infants read *Titch* by Pat Hutchins.
• For junior children read the growing and shrinking scene from *Alice in Wonderland* by Lewis Carroll.

True values

Money and shops are both popular classroom topics because of the practical maths skills they involve. Such topics tend to emphasise monetary value, at a time when children are all too keen to assess value in terms of money. The rest of the assemblies in this chapter are designed to encourage children to think of value in other ways.

10. Money

Assembly type
Infant classroom assembly.

What you need
Dogger by Shirley Hughes, one of your possessions which is very special to you.

What to do

This assembly focuses on the idea that something may appear to be only worth a few pence while being beyond value to the person who loves it.

Read *Dogger* to the children and focus the discussion on how the old toy was worth different things to different people. Comment on how the big blue teddy looked expensive and how it was of more monetary value than Dogger, but Dave valued Dogger more. Ask the children to talk about toys they love but wouldn't sell because they are worth so much to them. Show them one of your personal possessions which is very dear to you.

Prayer/reflection

Ask the children to think quietly about something which is precious to them and which they would never sell.

Song/hymn

Come and Praise
32 Thank you, Lord (adapt the words to include some of the objects you have mentioned)
17 Think of a world without any flowers
10 God who made the earth

11. What's it worth?

Assembly type

Infant school assembly.

What you need

Copy of photocopiable page 189.

What to do

Read the assembly story on page 189 to the children.

Prayer/reflection

Ask the children to think quietly about something which is precious to them and which they would never sell.

Song/hymn

Come and Praise
32 Thank you, Lord (adapt the words to include some of the objects you have mentioned)
17 Think of a world without any flowers
10 God who made the earth

Further activity

Discuss with the children the idea that some things and pets may be beyond value to their owners.

12. The rich man and Guru Nanak

Assembly type
Junior assembly, based on a Sikh story.

What you need
Picture of Guru Nanak, a needle, seven flags, copy of photocopiable page 190.

What to do
Before the assembly, make a display of the picture of Guru Nanak, the needle and the flags.

Tell the assembly story on page 190, pointing to the display at the appropriate moments.

Prayer/reflection
Listen to these sayings about money:
The best things in life are free.
You can't take it with you when you go.
All that glitters is not gold.
(Add any others that you or the children know.)

Song/hymn
'Can't buy me love' by the Beatles.

13. What is something worth?

Assembly type
Infant and junior school assembly

What you need
Copy of photocopiable page 191.

What to do
Adapt the assembly story on page 191 to your own style.

Prayer/reflection
Ask the children to think about what each brother gained and lost.

Further activities
• Ask older children to write a diary entry, imagining that they are either Jacob or Esau on the day of the sale. Encourage them to express feelings rather than just to give a straight forward chronological account of the events.
• Read 'Swops' from *Please Mrs. Butler* by Allan Ahlberg. Discuss why the child wouldn't swop his Mars Bars.

CHAPTER 6

Classroom worship

Classroom-based worship allows intimacy which is lost with the larger numbers of a whole- or half-school assembly. There can be a closer and more immediate link between the activities and a time of worship, and more discussion is possible.

Books can be used, the illustrations of which would be lost with the distance created by a larger crowd, and the assemblies can be more finely tuned to the needs of the children. There are other examples of classroom-based worship throughout the book, where they are linked to subject-specific programmes of study. Many of the following assemblies are based on books which we suggest you read to the children, and they offer a pattern for using books as a lead-in to classroom worship.

1. The end of the day

Assembly type
An end-of-day act of worship which can be used on a daily basis.

What you need
A cassette recorder and tape of reflective music (optional), examples of the children's work done during the day, a picture book or a favourite poem.

What to do
The end of the day can be a time of gathering in, reflecting on the day, and saying good-bye until tomorrow. It can be the school's equivalent of the peaceful evening service of Compline. Begin the act of worship with a short session of singing or by listening to a tape.

Ask the children to recollect what they have done during the day and to name something they were pleased with. Look at items of the children's work and say thank you to children who have worked hard and contributed well. Remember together any children who are ill, or away from the class for a long period. Encourage the children to look forward to the next day. Include a picture book which invites reflection (see Bibliography, page 192 for suggestions). The book may well be an old favourite rather than always something new. As it is a time of reflection, the reading should invite an empathetic response rather than there being a discussion of particular words for meaning, or the like. Alternatively a favourite poem might be recited or a new one read.

Song/hymn
Sing together again and/or listen to music.

Prayer/reflection
Say together one of the 'Benedictions' or a combination of them (see Prayer, page 29). Regular repetition of the prayer or reflection over a number of days will enable the children to join in.

2. Jealousy

Assembly type
Classroom book-based assembly for nursery and infant children which could be linked into a topic on Myself, Feelings or Families.

What you need
Noisy Nora by Rosemary Wells.

What to do
Ask the children to shut their eyes and remember a time when they felt very angry with someone else, or think of the sort of things that make them feel cross.

Invite them to say something about it if they want to. Then read the story of *Noisy Nora* to the children. With this book there is a temptation to draw the moral that all children are loved equally by their parents, but sadly this is not always the case. Some children may identify with Nora in that they too feel loved after neglect.

Others will not. The strength of the story lies in its illustration of family feelings.

Ask the children to comment on Nora's feelings and why she felt that way.

Prayer/reflection
Say, 'We've thought about being angry with someone. Now let's think about being happy with that person.'

Song/hymn
Come and Praise
68 Kum ba yah (add verses, 'Someone's angry', and 'Someone's happy')

3. Grandparents

Assembly type
A short classroom assembly for nursery children and infants preceded by a series of preparatory activities which could be part of a topic on Families. It could also link to studies in science on growth, or to the history syllabus.

Stage 1 – Preparation

What you need
Painting or drawing equipment, materials for making a class book (such as stapler, a hole punch and some thread), books describing grandparents (such as *The Patchwork Quilt* by Valerie Flournoy, *A Balloon for Grandad* by Nigel Gray or *George's Marvellous Medicine* by Roald Dahl), a visit from someone who is a grandparent.

What to do

Begin a classroom discussion about grandparents, including collecting lots of the different names by which they are called (for example, nanna, gran, opa).

In this discussion it should be acknowledged that:
• some children don't have grandparents;
• some children may have been recently bereaved by the death of a grandparent, and feel sad about it;
• grandparents can often live far away;
• not everyone likes their grandparents, though there is often love between the two generations.

Reference could be made to *George's Marvellous Medicine* by Roald Dahl. Read *A Balloon for Grandad* to the children.

Ask the children to paint or draw pictures of a grandparent – or someone else's grandparent if they have none of their own. Ask them to caption the picture with statements about the grandparent, for example, what the grandparent likes or liked doing, what the child likes or liked doing with them, what he or she has taught the child. Make a book of the pictures and include one done by yourself.

Read *The Patchwork Quilt* by Valerie Flournoy to older infant children. Discuss with them the characters in the book and the feelings for the grandmother.

Raise with the children the question of whether all grannies are old people who sit still most of the day and have fragile health. Do some of the their grandparents go out to work? Look at some of the pictures of other grandparents doing things actively with their grandchildren (for example, in *Lucy and Tom's Christmas* by Shirley Hughes, the grandfather takes Tom out in the snow).

Invite a member of staff or a friend in the local community who is a grandparent to come into the class and talk about his or her grandchildren.

Stage 2 – Assembly

What you need

The class book about grandparents (see Preparation), a candle.

What to do

Bring the children together and ask individuals to read their page from the 'grandparents' book. Make it clear that the rest of the book can be read when it is in the class library.

Prayer/reflection

Light a candle and invite the class to think about children who have no grandparents or who feel sad because a grandparent is no longer with them. Say together a loud 'three cheers' for grandparents.

Song/hymn

Come and Praise
32 Thank you, Lord (adapt the words to include 'grandparents', and some of the things that the children have mentioned about their grandparents)

4. Do you believe in magic?

Assembly type

Book-based infant and lower junior class assembly.

What you need

Do You Believe in Magic? by Saviour Pirotta, a large curved shell.

What to do

Read *Do You Believe in Magic?* to the children. This book speaks for itself about the power of imagination and longing.

Pass the shell to a child and ask her to say what she hears in it and what picture that brings to mind. Invite other children to add to the picture in the way the children do in the book.

Prayer/reflection

Invite the children to listen in an imaginary shell and visualise being in a place where they would like to be.

Song/hymn
Come and Praise
60 I listen and I listen

Further activity
Ask the children to paint what they hear in the shell, if possible using the same ink and wash techniques as the artist.

5. A walking meditation

Assembly type
An outdoor class assembly for all ages in which the activity and the reflection combine to be the 'act of worship'.

What you need
No special equipment.

What to do
Take the children outside, preferably to a grassy area of the playground or a local park. Point out an item in the playground, such as a tree or a fence, and tell the children, that you want them to run to that place and back again as fast as they can. On their return, ask them to form a circle, and then tell you what sounds they noticed and what they saw. Why was it difficult to notice things?

Ask the children to breathe in and out slowly and deeply. Explain that this should help them to become relaxed and still. Now ask them to walk round in a circle very, very slowly and silently, placing one foot in front of the other with great deliberation. After they have been moving a short time ask them to listen for as many sounds as they can while they are walking. Then ask them to look around them and think about the things they are noticing as they are walking.

Sit down in the circle together and discuss quietly what the children have seen and heard.

Song/hymn
Come and Praise
60 I listen and I listen
96 A still small voice

The Snowman

The film version of Raymond Briggs' *The Snowman* is quite ethereal. The quality of music and the drawings can elicit the sense of awe and wonder which is part of the experience of worship. For many children the film offers a similar experience to that which some adults have when listening to a beautiful choir in a magnificent cathedral. However, it has a number of themes within it

which can be used as a springboard for further experience and discussion. We have outlined some here.

While it would be best to obtain a copy of the video and to replay parts of the film, this is not always easy to organise. If using a video is not feasible, the original book is a useful substitute.

The following series of activities are based on the video, and are designed for classroom assemblies for the five to nine age range.

6. Feelings

What you need
A copy of *The Snowman* video, soft pastel crayons or other drawing materials, paper.

What to do
Watch the video of *The Snowman* together.

Ask the children to choose a scene from the video and draw it, then talk about the scene they have drawn to their neighbour. Ask a few children to show their drawings to the rest of the class. Encourage them to talk about the feelings of the child in the film and to express how the different scenes made them feel.

Prayer/reflection
Listen to some of the happy music from *The Snowman* video. Ask the children to think of a scene that it reminds them of. Listen to some of the sad music. Again, ask the children to think of a scene.

7. Being alone

What you need
A video of *The Snowman* or a copy of the book.

What to do
Start by reading to the children the words of the following nursery rhyme:
'Here I am
Little Jumping Joan
When nobody is with me
I am all alone.'

Play the opening scene of *The Snowman* or look at the book. Draw out from the children the isolation of the boy in the film. Discuss with them when they like to be alone and when they long to be with friends. Share with them your own experiences as a child.

Being alone can be a very pleasant time of contentment, or it can be lonely and even frightening. Encourage children to express both, if that is true to their own experience.

Encourage the children to join in the nursery rhyme with you.

Prayer/reflection
Let us think of children who feel lonely:
Children who live a long way from others;
Children starting at a new school where they feel lonely;
Children whose friends are all away from them.

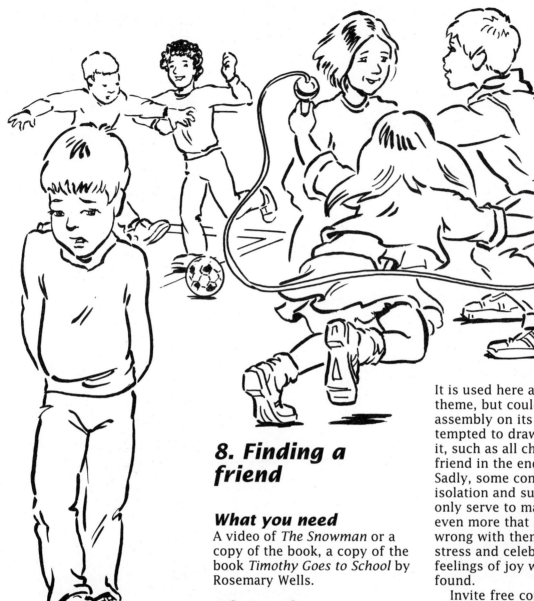

8. Finding a friend

What you need

A video of *The Snowman* or a copy of the book, a copy of the book *Timothy Goes to School* by Rosemary Wells.

What to do

Play the relevant part of the video including the parts where the snowman and child enjoy themselves being mischievous in the house, or look at the book.

Tell the children you are going to read another book about a child making a friend. Read *Timothy Goes to School* which powerfully expresses both loneliness and friendship.

It is used here as part of the theme, but could easily be an assembly on its own. Don't be tempted to draw a moral from it, such as all children finding a friend in the end, as not all do. Sadly, some continue in isolation and such comments only serve to make them feel even more that something is wrong with them. Instead stress and celebrate the feelings of joy when a friend is found.

Invite free comment afterwards from the class about the feelings of the children in the film and the book. Encourage them to remember times when they made a new friend, and to talk about the things they enjoy doing with friends.

Prayer/reflection

Three cheers for friends everywhere.

Song/hymn

Come and Praise
65 When I needed a neighbour
68 Kum ba yah

Further activity

Children could draw a picture of themselves alone, and either talk or write about it.

Song/hymn
Come and Praise
32 Thank you, Lord (adapt the words to include 'all our friends')

9. The wonder of nature

What you need
Video or book of *The Snowman*, paper, crayons or pencils, boards, a selection of natural objects such as flowers or rocks or shells.

What to do
Look at the episodes from *The Snowman* which depict the outside world. Several scenes in the film celebrate the natural world; the whale, the penguins, the snow scenes and the night sky. Explain how artists watch the world and animals very carefully so they can paint them and show their pleasure in them. This act of artistic creation can in itself be an act of worship.

Go outside with the children and ask them to draw a natural scene, even if it is just a bare tree in a city environment or the sky on a stormy day. If the weather is unsuitable for this, let the children stay in the classroom and draw natural objects, such as flowers, rocks or shells.

Encourage the children to share and enjoy their pictures together.

Song/hymn
Come and Praise
1 Morning has broken
3 All things bright and beautiful
4 Autumn days
11 For the beauty of the earth
12 Who put the colours in the rainbow?

Further activity
Build up a display of artists' drawings of animals.

10. The celebration

Stage 1 – Preparation

What you need
A video of *The Snowman*, coloured paper, scissors, stapler, ingredients for making party food.

What to do
This activity does not follow the usual form of an assembly, but the act of group celebration, which draws the community together, is very

close to worship. Show the children the party scene from *The Snowman* and discuss with them the idea of celebrating with friends. Let them help you plan a party. Provide them with appropriate materials and ask them to make party hats.

Let them help you to make party food or arrange for food to be brought in on the day.

Stage 2 – Assembly/celebration

What you need
A recording of *The Snowman Suite* by Howard Blake, party food and paper hats (see Preparation), a large space for dancing.

What to do
Play the dance music from *The Snowman* and let the children do simple dances together as in the film, for example skipping round in circles, moving in and out in circles, dancing in pairs while linking right arms then left arms. Let the children wear their party hats if they wish. When the music is finished, let the children help themselves to the party food. Before they settle down to eat, say the following grace, 'Let us celebrate friendship, let us be thankful for this food.'

11. Farewell to friendships

What you need
The Snowman book and a recording of *The Snowman Suite*, cassette player, a candle, matches, a low table, a large space.

What to do

Most children, even very young ones, have experienced the loss of a friend, classmate or teacher through someone moving house or school. This session gives them the chance to talk about that experience as well as the opportunity to share the pain of the child in the film. Again it is important not to draw a moral because not all friendships do end with a sense of loss. Some continue until old age; others fizzle out naturally.

Retell the story using the music and ask the children to dance or mime to each section, encouraging them to convey the moods rather that imitate the action. At the end of the music, ask the children to sit in a circle. Invite them to talk about friends they no longer see. Light the candle and place it on a low table. Ask the children to name some of those friends, including any children and teachers who have left the school.

Prayer/reflection

We remember and give thanks for all friendships.
We give thanks for the ones which only lasted a short time.
We think about those friends who have gone away.
We give thanks for the friends we have now.

Ask the children to give three cheers for friendship.

Song/hymn
Come and Praise
11 For the beauty of the earth
32 Thank you, Lord (adapt the words to include 'all our friends')

Further activity

Read 'Teddy Robinson and the Beautiful Present' in *About Teddy Robinson* by Joan Robinson. This takes up the theme of that something can be of value even if only brief in duration.

CHAPTER 7

Festivals

The major festivals of the Christian faith are the highlights of the Church's calendar, the peak of its worship. Churches are packed at Christmas, Easter and Harvest when Christians celebrate their faith and confirm their commitment to it in ritual and music. Each year they tell again the story of Christ's birth, his death and resurrection, and at harvest they affirm a belief in God as the Lord of Creation.

But what of the place of Christian festivals in schools? Schools are not Christian communities, so is there a place for the celebrations of these festivals? Clearly, these festivals have traditionally played a major role; perhaps because, whatever the individual beliefs of staff and children, this country is culturally Christian, as the 1988 Act recognises. The secular community has appropriated the Christian festivals for its own use, just as the Church originally appropriated the festivals of earlier belief systems. So at Eastertime, the rebirth of spring is celebrated by Christian and non-Christian alike. Similarly at Christmas, family and children are celebrated, as is the concept of light in the darkness. Christians, however, give such beliefs a theistic context. The celebration of these festivals in secular schools is thus often a celebration of the beliefs shared across the community.

BACKGROUND

So what of other faiths? It is possible to study the festivals of various faiths in schools in a practical way, for example tasting the appropriate food, hearing the stories and learning about the acts of worship. Such a study could be used for children learning about the various faiths practised in Britain, as the Act requires. However, in our view these festivals cannot be genuinely celebrated in the context of an act of worship, unless there is a substantial presence of members of the faith concerned in the school. Then it may be that they can celebrate the festival and invite others to share their celebrations, in the same way as non-believers often share in the celebration of marriage in a church without sharing the belief in God. They celebrate, but do not do so in a full religious sense. This offers a further model of what happens in the celebration of Christmas and Easter in schools where there is a substantially committed Christian presence.

When, though, there are no members of a particular faith in the school, celebration does not seem a suitable word. Such a description can even cause offence because members of one faith may not want their children celebrating the beliefs of another, although they may be quite happy for them to learn about them. Conversely it can be seen to be a denigration of the festival by members of the faith concerned if it can be celebrated so lightly.

Nevertheless, festivals can form the basis of a school or class assembly in three different ways, without being an actual celebration of that festival. Below are three possible forms for such assemblies which can be adapted to suit the age and group size of the children concerned. We have not given details on specific festivals as such information is readily available in many books (see Bibliography page 192).

However, we have given a list of the key underlying themes of some of the major festivals in different faiths. As these are usually movable feasts we have only given the time of year not the date.

1. The fact of celebration

What you need
The story behind the chosen festival and any central features of its celebration, relevant music, artefacts and pictures.

What to do
Tell the children that in Britain and/or the local community, people of the appropriate faith are celebrating this festival. Describe the rituals in general terms, tell the children the story behind the festival, and why it is being celebrated. When the children are familiar with the festival, let them describe it in assembly, perhaps acting out the story to the whole school.

Alternatively you could invite a member of the faith to come and talk about the festival to the school.

Prayer/reflection
Ask the children to shout in a very loud voice 'Happy...', trying to make their wishes heard by all the people of that faith in Britain! Repeat this twice, encouraging them to shout more loudly each time.

Further activities
• If the festival is celebrated locally, suggest that the children make cards with best wishes for the festival and send these to the appropriate place of worship.
• Encourage the children to find out more about the festival, then let them make some of the appropriate food.

2. Focusing on a theme

What you need
No special equipment.

What to do
Tell the children that the festival is being celebrated in the faith community, but focus on one of the underlying themes of the festival and translate that into terms relevant to the children's experience. For example, as Chinese New Year focuses on making the New Year a lucky one, have the children identify what they think makes up a year of good fortune.

Prayer/reflection

Say some words which reflect the theme of the festival.

3. A celebration of light

What you need

Songs and stories from the three festivals, a Divali lamp, a Hannukah menorah, a Christingle or Christingles for the whole class.

What to do

This is an example of an assembly drawing together festivals with a common theme. This particular assembly could be linked to a topic on Light. The beginning of winter brings, in rapid succession, three festivals with a theme of Light: the Hindu festival of Divali, the Jewish festival of Hannukah and the Christian festival of Christmas.

In class beforehand, teach the children a story and a song about light from each festival. Alternatively, different classes could study one festival each.

For the assembly itself make sure the hall lights are as dim as possible.

Begin with a child making a speech of welcome and explaining the common connection of light between the three festivals. Then let three children explain the connection with light for each of the faiths.

• During Divali people put lamps in their windows to welcome home Rama and Sita.

• The candles of the Jewish menorah are lit during Hannukah because the holy light stayed burning for eight days when there was only enough oil to burn for one night, thus symbolising God's power over evil and darkness.

• At Christmas some Christians make 'Christingles' to demonstrate their belief that Christ came as a light to a dark world. The Christingle is a candle stuck into an orange. The orange represents the world, the candle the light of Christ. A red ribbon round the orange represents the blood of Christ and dried fruit and peanuts stuck on cocktail sticks are the fruits of the Spirit.

After each explanation, let the class sing an appropriate song. If it is within the safety regulations of your local authority, turn off the lights and have one or more children enter in a procession, carrying the lit Christingles as they sing a carol.

Prayer/reflection

As the procession ends, allow for a few seconds of silence before saying:
May light overcome the darkness.
May love overcome hate.
May hope overcome fear.
May we learn to live in peace with one another. Amen.

Festivals and their themes

January/February
Chinese New Year: new beginnings, saying good-bye to the bad things of a previous year, hoping for a good year.

March/April
Easter (Christian): new life, death and resurrection, spring, good and evil, suffering overcoming evil.
Passover (Jewish): slavery and freedom, remembrance.
Holi (Hindu): harvest, games.

April
Baisakhi (Sikh): the struggle for one's faith, fighting against injustice.

September/October
Jewish New Year: repentance, new beginnings.

October/November
Divali (Hindu/Sikh): new beginnings, light, good and evil, harvest.

December
Christmas (Christian): light in the midst of darkness, birth of a baby, gifts.
Hannukah (Jewish): light, good and evil, the struggle for one's faith.

Muslim festivals
The dates of Muslim festivals are fixed according to a lunar calendar, and so move approximately eleven days earlier each year. We therefore do not give a date for these:
Eid-ul-fitr: thanksgiving for food and for God's goodness, self-discipline
Eid-ul-adha: pilgrimage, the struggle for one's faith.

PHOTOCOPIABLES

The pages in this section can be photocopied and adapted to your own needs and those of your class; they do not need to be declared in respect of any photocopying licence. Some of the pages can be used as handouts for use in the classroom, while others provide stories or poems to be read out in assembly. Each photocopiable page relates to a specific assembly in the main body of the book. The appropriate assembly and page references are given with each photocopiable sheet.

Father, page 20

HAVE YOU SEEN THIS PERSON?

You feel peaceful when you're w...
you would obey because he or...
rules, is kind and loving, wou...
when you were afraid or feeli...
you had done something wr...

Islamic

A bird dance, page 64

The bird and the crumb

A bird came down the walk:
He did not know I saw;
He bit an angle-worm in halves
And ate the fellow, raw.

And then he drank the dew
From a convenient grass,
And then hopped sideways to the wall
To let a beetle pass.

He glanced with rapid eyes
That hurried all abroad,
They looked like frightened beads, I thought.
He stirred his velvet head

Like one in danger; cautious,
I offered him a crumb,
And he unrolled his feathers
And rowed him softer home

Than oars divide the ocean,
Too silver for a seam,
Or butterflies, off banks of noon,
Leap, splashless, as they swim.

Emily Dickinson

Greek

Πάτερ ἡμῶν ὁ ἐν τοῖζ οὐρανοῖζ, ἁγιασθήτω τὸ ὄνομά σου

Pater hemoon ho en tois ouranois agiasthetoo to onoma sou.

Latin

Pater noster, qui es in caelis, sanctificetur nomen tuum.

King James Bible

Our Father, which art in Heaven, hallowed be Thy name.

Long, long ago, after Jesus had lived on earth, the first Christians met together to talk about their faith in Jesus. They would share some bread together and pass wine around and, when they did this, they remembered how Jesus ate and drank his last meal with them and thought about how they missed him. They told each other stories about what he used to say and do and when they had a problem, they thought about what Jesus might have said about it. When they wanted to pray, they remembered the prayer that Jesus taught them. Of course, they didn't pray it in English but in their own language, the language Jesus spoke, called Aramaic. Nobody is quite sure now exactly what Aramaic was like, so we will just imagine them praying in their own language.

Many people became Christians who weren't from Palestine but from other countries. Although they spoke different languages, they could usually speak Greek. Some time after Jesus's death, the first Christians were worried about forgetting the things he had said, so they wrote them down, and when they did, they wrote in Greek. So the first copies of the Lord's Prayer were in Greek. It went like this.

(*Read the Greek text and ask the children to say it after you.*)

Over time, however, the Christian message spread through many countries and the common language was no longer Greek but Latin. Whatever language people spoke at home, they used Latin in church. So the Lord's Prayer was translated into Latin.

(*Read the text and ask the children to say it after you.*)

Centuries passed. Some people were content to go on saying the Lord's Prayer in Latin, and the few people who could read, read the Bible in Latin. But others said they wanted to be able to read it in their own language. In Germany, a man called Martin Luther translated the Bible into German, and in England people started to translate it into English. In 1604 King James ordered that an English translation of the whole Bible be made. It was finished in 1611, and in many churches people started to pray the words of the Lord's Prayer in English.

(*Read with the children the words of the King James version.*)

Since then, there have been translations of the Lord's Prayer into hundreds of other languages, and there have been new translations into English. In most churches people use a newer translation, but the King James one is still very popular.

HAVE YOU SEEN THIS PERSON ?

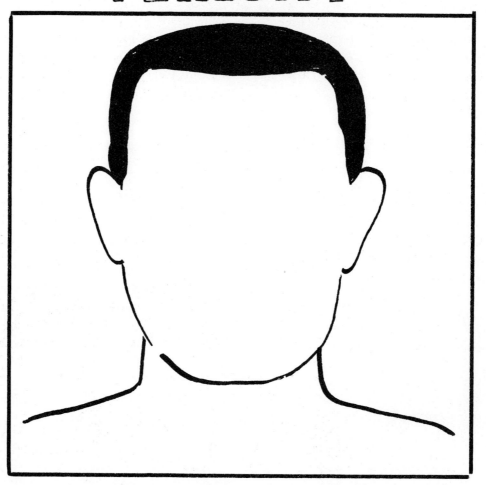

You feel peaceful when you're with him or her, you would obey because he or she made wise rules, is kind and loving, would comfort you when you were afraid or feeling bad because you had done something wrong.

Jesus was an itinerant preacher. He went about the countryside teaching anyone who would listen to him. He taught his followers many things, but above all he taught them about God. He explained God's characteristics: God is loving and kind; God is wise and so makes good rules for people to obey; God comforts people when they are afraid or feel bad because they have done something wrong. When Jesus was talking about God, he told stories and used images to help people understand. So he said that God was like a council official who will listen when someone pesters him, or like a shepherd who cares for each one of his sheep, or like someone giving a party who is upset if people don't come. But, above all, he said that God was like a father; not a father who was grumpy sometimes as most human fathers are; not a father who got cross because he was tired from work, or a father who was unfair as human fathers sometimes are; no, he told his listeners that God was a perfect father who was always kind and loving, made wise rules and was forgiving. So when Jesus taught his followers to pray to God, he told them to start by saying 'Our Father'. Actually, we know that he often used the word 'Abba', which translates into English better as 'Daddy' which seems much more loving and friendly than 'father', doesn't it?

Christians, the followers of Jesus, continue to call God 'Father'. Some Christians, though, say that God is not only like a good father but also like a good mother, who encourages and comforts you. Others say that God is like a good mother and also like a good friend.

What is heaven like and what did Jesus mean when he talked about God being in heaven? Let's think about that today.

Some people think about heaven as a place above the clouds and they draw pictures of God as an old man looking down at the earth.

Lots of cartoons show heaven as being a place where people sit round on clouds, wearing white robes and strumming harps.

In the Muslim holy book, the Qur'an, heaven is described as a beautiful, sunny garden where there are lots of trees to give shade. The trees are heavily laden with the most delicious fruit (Sura 56:27-40).

Some children imagine heaven as a place where they never have to go to school and sweets grow on trees. Presumably, they think that the sweets in heaven won't rot their teeth.

Other people say that heaven is a place where there is a big party going on with everyone joining in the great feast, or that it is a beautiful city where the streets are paved with gold.

Some people say it is where the heavenly creatures, such as angels, live.

Others say that they can't imagine what heaven is like, but they know that it will be perfect and will be filled with God's glory. Everyone will be kind and love each other.

Others say they don't know what heaven is like, but they believe it is a place of happy reunions, where people go when they die and meet those people they have loved who have died before them.

Some say that there is no such place as heaven.

Some say that heaven doesn't exist yet, but one day the earth will become perfect and heaven will exist on earth.

So there are lots and lots of different ideas about heaven. Which one is right? We can't tell, can we?

But what did Jesus believe about heaven? That's difficult to know. Some people think that Jesus thought that a physical place called heaven existed; a place where God lives and rules. Others think that he was reminding his followers that he wasn't talking about earthly fathers but about God, who is everywhere not just on earth.

What do you think?

What has that poem got to do with 'Hallowed be thy name' or 'May your name be kept holy'? Well, in times past and still today, people do wrong things in God's name. They kill others for the sake of religion. They use the excuse 'Well, God told me to do it', rather like the child in the poem said, 'But Jonathan told me to do it'. People also used to write the name of God on pieces of paper, or, in the time of Jesus on cloth or papyrus, and try to do magic spells with it, because they believed God's name was so powerful. That's one reason why many Jews today still won't write the name of God in full on paper.

They don't want to run the risk that someone will take the name that they have written and do evil with it. They also want to show their respect for God.

Jesus was a Jew. When he said that God's name should be hallowed, and kept holy, he was saying, 'Don't let people do evil in God's name. Keep God's name out of things which are wrong. Don't use God as an excuse.'

We have been listening to profiles of earthly rulers. Some of them have very little power, some of them have a lot. Some have positions of authority because they have been elected by the people, while some have got there by brute force.

At the time when Jesus was teaching and preaching, his country, Palestine, was ruled by the Romans. Everywhere you went there were Roman soldiers. The people had to pay very heavy taxes to the Romans. The taxes were not spent on schools and hospitals and to help the community, as they are in many countries today. No, they were spent on the upkeep of the Roman army and some of the money was sent back to the Emperor in Rome. The Romans had helped a man called Herod to rule as king of Judea. Herod did just what the Romans wanted him to do. That's why he is known as a puppet king. He was like a puppet who jumped when the Romans 'pulled the strings'. It was no wonder that the Jews loathed Herod just as they loathed the Romans who dominated their land. They longed for someone to lead a rebellion and crush the Romans.

It seems that some people thought that Jesus might be that man. They heard him preach about God's kingdom and they saw how people listened to him. But Jesus refused to become a rebel leader who would use force to set up his own kingdom. He said constantly that what he was concerned about was God's kingdom not human rule. So in the prayer he taught his followers, he prayed for God's kingdom and God's rule to come on earth. We will look at what sort of kingdom that was to be in the next assembly.

The question still remains: Where is God's kingdom? Many of the first Christians waited for God's kingdom to come on earth, for a time when all the sick would be healed, the lame walk and the poor be poor no longer. But nothing seemed to happen. Then some Christians began to think differently. They said that God never forced His rule on anyone. He wouldn't come and conquer the earth and make people do as He said. Instead, they believed that God's kingdom was wherever people obeyed God's laws. It was wherever people tried to love God with their hearts, souls and spirits and love others as much as they loved themselves. Today, as in the past, Christians and people from other faiths work for the needy in the world because they believe that this is what God wants: that His kingdom is wherever people help the poor.

But not all Christians think the same way. Some think that God's kingdom is only in the future, in heaven, in the life after this one.

In Palestine where Jesus lived, bread was the staple food. If you had had some bread you felt as if you had eaten properly, even if you had eaten little else. So it was often used as a symbol for all that was nourishing and life-giving.

For poor people, bread was particularly important. Jesus was a poor man. He went about the countryside preaching, teaching and healing. He had to rely on other people to give food to him and his twelve closest followers, the disciples, because he couldn't grow his own food and wasn't earning money in the usual way. Sometimes he must have wondered where the next day's food was coming from. Once, when he and his disciples were very hungry, he sent them into a field to gather up the grains of corn left behind after the harvest, as the poor were allowed to do. It was not an easy life for them.

So when Jesus taught his followers to pray, he told them to tell God about their most basic need, bread for that day. He told them to say, 'Give us this day, our daily bread.'

Jesus was a Jew. When they did have bread, he would have given thanks for it according to the Jewish custom. He might have said something in Aramaic, very similar to that which Jews say today, 'You are blessed, Lord our God, the sovereign of the world who brings forth bread into the world'.

In giving thanks, he was showing that he didn't take bread for granted. He was always grateful for it, and indeed for all food.

Today many people, all over the world, do not know where their next meal is coming from. They might live in places which are hot and dry, where nothing has grown because there is no water, which we call a drought, or they might live in places where there is too much water, where torrential rain and flooding has broken down the crops, sweeping away all before it. People might live in places which have been ravaged by war, causing famine. Or they might have fled from cruel soldiers to live in refugee camps where there is not enough land to support all the people and there is no money to buy food. They are dependent on people in other countries, like Britain, to help them. Most days they get up and say to themselves, 'Please, please let there be something for my child to eat.' And that's another way of saying, 'Give us today, our daily bread,' as it says in the Lord's Prayer.

Jesus taught his followers to forgive their enemies and to be kind to those who hurt them. He reminded them that they too sometimes did things which were wrong and hurtful. He also told them that they should be like children in some things. Perhaps forgiving was one of those things, as children are often both better and quicker at making up after quarrels than adults. Often when children say, 'I'm never going to talk to you again,' they are very best friends again the next day.

Sometimes, however, children can be too forgiving. Sometimes adults or older children can hurt them and then they need to go and talk about what's happened with someone they trust, rather than being forgiving and saying that it doesn't matter really.

When Jesus taught his followers the Lord's Prayer, he told them to say, 'Please forgive me, God, in the same way that I forgive those who hurt me.'

In the translation of the Lord's Prayer that we are looking at, the words are, 'Forgive us our trespasses as we forgive those who trespass against us.' The words mean, 'Please forgive us God, in the same way that we forgive those who hurt us.'

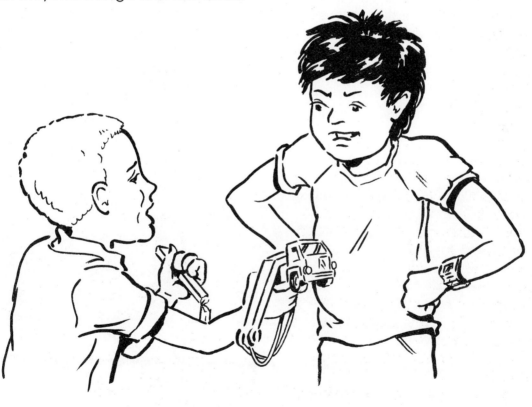

Jesus and his followers thought that there was going to be a time which would be so terrible that people would wish they had never been born. There would be wars and rumours of wars, there would be much bloodshed and there would be much pain. They hoped and hoped that it would never happen, from the bottom of their hearts they prayed that it wouldn't. But they also hoped and hoped that if it did happen, they would be able cope with it.

In fact, there was a bad war in Palestine about 30 years after the death of Jesus. There was a rebellion which the Romans crushed severely. Many Jews and Christians were persecuted by the Romans, but they went on praying to God that they wouldn't lose their faith in him, and that they would come through the awful time, in the words of the Lord's Prayer, that they would be delivered from evil. The early Christians added some words to what Jesus said, to emphasise this even further. They said, 'For thine is the kingdom, the power and the glory, for ever and ever,' to emphasise and remind themselves that in the long run God's kingdom would come and the evil time would end.

Today many people, including children, have fears and anxieties about things; for some it is about wars, others are worried about what will happen to their own lives. They say to themselves or to God, 'Please don't let it happen, and if the worst happens, please may I get through it.' The words in the Lord's Prayer, 'Do not bring us to temptation, but deliver us from evil,' are another way of expressing that wish.

Sometimes it can be very hard to sit still and quiet, especially if you've been racing round outside, can't it? It can be even harder if you've quarrelled with someone and are still seething with anger. All you can think about is how cross you are with them. It can also be hard if you are feeling very anxious, because all your worries keep buzzing round your head.

Some people, when they feel like that, use music to help them feel calm, either by listening to it or by concentrating on playing it. Others paint or do some embroidery. Many people of all sorts of different religions use prayers to help them keep still and be calm. They sometimes take a string of beads (*take the beads in your hand to demonstrate*) and say a prayer, holding on to each bead in turn. Many Christians pray the Lord's Prayer this way. They use it to help them be still and calm and think about God.

Instead of using beads, you can also use your fingers.

(*Invite the children to copy you. Act as if you are counting on your fingers, but instead of saying numbers say one line of the Lord's Prayer on each one.*)

It doesn't matter how you break the lines. When you run out of fingers just start again.

So, as well as praying the Lord's Prayer in church or school, people have prayed it at home to help them be still and remember God. Over the last few weeks we've been trying to give meaning to the Lord's Prayer and that's important, but Christians have also found that just saying it without always thinking about the words can also be a way of being with God.

There once was a wise man, a philosopher called Diogenes. He was born in Greece about 400 years before Jesus was born. When Diogenes was young, he went to the city of Athens to enjoy the exciting city life. He wore the best clothes, lived in the most comfortable house and went to many parties.

But he soon became bored by this and wandered out to listen to the great teachers – the philosophers for which Athens was famous. He listened to many different ones, but one of them he found really interesting. This man's name was Antisthenes. He taught that all things such as wealth, pleasure, fine clothes and so on, were useless. Only honesty and truth were important. Diogenes found him fascinating and soon he was following the teachings of Antisthenes. Diogenes wore only the roughest clothes. He slept at first just on the bare earth, but later found that a big empty barrel was even better. He lived in this barrel for some time.

One day he went on a ship to visit some friends. The ship was captured by pirates and Diogenes was sold as a slave to a wise man who lived in the city of Corinth. Soon Diogenes's master realised what a wonderful man he had bought. He gave Diogenes his freedom and Diogenes stayed on in his house to teach the children.

While he was in Corinth, Diogenes met one of the most famous men of all time – Alexander the Great.

Alexander the Great is famous for being a conqueror. He died when he was 32 but by then he had led his armies to conquer Greece, Persia, Egypt, Afghanistan and parts of India. He was strong, clever and powerful.

One day he came to Corinth, not as an ordinary visitor but as a conqueror. His army had fought the Corinthian army and won. Now his soldiers were storming through the streets. But Alexander had heard of Diogenes's wisdom and he had told his soldiers, 'Find the house of the philosopher Diogenes. Make sure no-one harms it. Put a guard outside, and bring a message to me at once. I want to meet this man.'

At first Diogenes refused to see him, but Alexander was so persistent that at last the philosopher agreed.

Alexander strode across the courtyard to the little hut where Diogenes lived. He stooped at the doorway and looked inside. There was Diogenes sitting on the ground.

'Old man, wise Diogenes,' he said, 'I am Alexander. The world is at my command. What can I do for you?'

There was a long silence.

Eventually Diogenes looked up at Alexander, the most powerful man in the world, and said, 'Yes, there is one thing you can do. Please move out of the doorway, you are blocking the sun.'

Alexander had met his match and went away muttering, 'If I were not Alexander, then I would be Diogenes.'

Once some rabbis sat complaining about the Roman occupation of their country, Palestine. 'I ask you,' proclaimed one loudly, 'what have the Romans ever done for us Jews? Nothing, I tell you. Nothing.'

There was silence as heads nodded in agreement.

But then a small voice piped up, 'Well, they have built all those wonderful baths, you know. They're beautifully warm, much better than bathing in the river.'

'Yes, yes, the baths,' replied the first impatiently. 'But if you don't count the baths, what else have they done for us? Absolutely nothing.' He beat his fist on the table to emphasise his point.

'There's the bridges. They've built the bridges,' said a third. 'It is much easier crossing many rivers now than it used to be when we had to rely on the ferry.'

But the first rabbi couldn't be convinced. 'O.K. There are the bridges, and the baths, I see that, but I still say, what have the Romans ever done for us?'

'What about the roads?' butted in another. 'They have built all those straight roads. It is much quicker getting from Jerusalem to Jericho than it used to be, and much less wear on the carts. No, they've built good roads for us.'

'And don't forget the market-places,' added someone else. 'They are much better than the old ones.'

It seemed the argument was lost. It seemed that the Romans had done a lot for the Jews. But then the wise Rabbi Simeon bar Yohai spoke up.

'Yes, the Romans have made improvements, but not for us. They have built the baths to clean their own bodies. They have built bridges so they can collect tolls from us when we pass over them. They have built roads so that their soldiers can move more quickly and keep us under control. They have built market-places to make it easy to buy and sell slaves. Whatever the Romans have done, they have done it for themselves, for their own wicked ends; they have done it for themselves and not for us.'

When the Roman governor heard that Rabbi Simeon had been speaking out against the Romans, he sentenced him to death. Freedom of speech and freedom to criticise were not allowed under Roman rule. So Rabbi Simeon fled, with his son, to safety in the hills in the stony desert.

Seeing these pictures of refugees helps us to understand what it may have been like when the Roman Empire collapsed, and city after city was overrun and destroyed by strangers from the north. St Jerome was a scholar who lived at that time. He had left his home and gone to live away from the busy world in a monastery in North Africa. There he planned to spend his time in study and translating the Bible so that people could read it more easily. But the world would not leave him in peace, for they were terrible times. He heard news that his home town had been destroyed, many of his relatives had died, and the family property had been reduced to ruins. He wrote, 'I shudder to think of the catastrophes of our time. For more than twenty years Roman blood has daily been shed... the Roman world is falling... If only I had a watch-tower so high as to view the whole earth, I would show you the wreck of a world.'

Eventually he had to give up his work on his books because there was more urgent work to be done. He was trying to write about the book of Ezekiel, but he wrote, 'There is no hour, almost no single moment, when we are not relieving crowds of refugees, and the quiet of the monastery has turned to the bustle of a guest-house. So much so that we had either to shut our doors to them or abandon the study of the Scriptures.... I am not boasting, as some may suspect, of the welcome given to the fugitives, but acknowledging the causes of delay. We did give up the exposition of Ezekiel, and almost all study, and were filled with a longing to turn the words of scripture into deeds, not just saying holy things but doing them. In addition to these hindrances, my eyes are growing dim with age.'

Jerome was seventy-two when he wrote that. It was hard for him to turn from the books he loved in order to care for the homeless, but he knew he could not go on writing about God, who loved the world, when there were people in God's world who desperately needed his help.

Caedmon sat in the cowshed, all alone except for the animals peacefully chewing the cud beside him. This was his place; the place where he could go to be alone when he was miserable, the place where no-one would laugh at him or look down on him. It was his job to look after the animals belonging to the great Abbey of Whitby, and at this time of night no-one would disturb him.

'Why don't I go back in?' he asked himself in despair. 'Everyone else is having a good time, singing and playing the harp and telling those wonderful stories, all in poetry. I could just creep in and sit in a corner where no-one would notice me.'

But he knew it wouldn't work. Every time when the harp was passed round the great hall, no matter how he tried to hide, someone would pass it to him.

'Come on, Caedmon, give us a song!' they would say, laughing. 'Tell a story, do something to entertain us! Everyone else has had a go! Don't be a spoilsport! Come on, your singing can't be that bad!'

'Oh yes it can!' joked another. 'Spare us, Caedmon, don't sing, whatever you do! Don't you know any comic verse? A story? Nothing? All right, lads, leave him alone, he can't help it. Pass the harp to me, Caedmon.'

They meant no harm, but Caedmon was miserable. He tried to remember the songs he heard, or make up verses with an exciting story, but when he opened his mouth his mind went blank and nothing came out but a croaking noise. So he sat alone in the cowshed, and wept.

'Dear God,' he prayed, 'I want to be able to sing. I want to make up beautiful poetry. I want it so much...' And with that thought in his mind, he fell asleep.

It seemed like no time at all before he realised he was not alone. A man stood beside him in the cowshed.

'Caedmon,' said the man, 'sing me a song.'

Caemon's heart sank. 'Oh, no,' he thought, 'have they come tormenting me here too?'

With a sob he replied, 'I can't sing – I can't, I can't! Why do you think I left the feast and came out here?'

'But you shall sing to me,' said the man, and there was something about him that made Caedmon think that maybe it wasn't impossible after all. He hesitated.

'What should I sing about?'

'Sing about the creation of things.'

Before he knew what was happening, Caedmon opened his mouth and began to sing. He sang words and tunes that he had never heard before, of a beauty that brought tears to his eyes even as he sang. He sang in praise of God who made heaven and earth; in praise of God whose loving power made all the world; in praise of God who had made men and women and given them the earth to live on; in praise of God who had clothed the earth with green things and with flowers.

When Caedmon awoke, he knew he had been dreaming. But the dream was so clear in his mind that he thought perhaps he could remember some of the song he had sung. 'I'll try,' he thought. 'It won't come out as beautiful as it was in the dream, because I know I can't sing. But I'll do what I can.' So he opened his mouth and began to sing, and to his delight he found that he was singing the song in praise of God, word for word, just as he had sung it in his dream! Full of joy, he set about his work in the stable, still singing to himself. It wasn't long before he noticed something else.

'That last verse I sang – that wasn't in my dream. That's a new verse! I'm singing a new song all the time. Thank you, God, that you have answered my prayer!'

Full of excitement, he went to see his master, the steward who looked after the abbey's farm. Caedmon told him about this wonderful gift that God had given him.

The steward listened to his song.

'Come straight away and see our Abbess Hilda,' he said. 'Our abbey has been greatly blessed!'

Abbess Hilda was famous all over the kingdom for her wisdom and her learning. She was in charge of both monks and nuns in this Abbey of Whitby, and she made sure that they were well educated and could read and explain the Bible and other Christian books. There were several bishops in the land who owed their training to Hilda of Whitby. She called together several of the most learned men and women that she knew, and before them came Caedmon, who could neither read nor write, and had never had the Bible explained to him, or heard any Bible stories.

Abbess Hilda and her learned advisers listened as Caedmon sang his songs again, and they too realised that God had given their abbey a great gift.

'Can you make up any more songs, Caedmon?' asked the Abbess Hilda.

'I don't know,' said Caedmon. 'I don't know what to sing about.'

'Listen then,' said Hilda. She read to Caedmon a passage from the Bible, and she explained to him what it meant, and what the Church taught about it. 'Now go,' she said, 'and put it into verse if you can.'

The next day Caedmon came back, and in front of Hilda and her advisers, he sang the most beautiful song about what he had learned. His hearers were moved to tears. 'Praise God who has given you such a gift!' said Hilda. 'We must look after your gift and develop it. Will you give up looking after the animals, and come into the Abbey? Will you become a monk, so that you can learn more about God, and turn what you know into songs that ordinary people can love and understand?'

So Caedmon became a monk, and it was like a new world opening up for him as he listened to his teachers. Everything he learned he stored up in his mind. When he had thought about it for some time, he turned it into such wonderful verse that those who had been teaching him became his audience, and listened entranced to his praise of God. He sang of the creation of the world, and of how God rescued His people from Egypt. He sang of Jesus's birth in Bethlehem, and his death on the cross. He sang of the followers of Jesus, and how they went out into the world to tell people that Jesus was alive.

Caedmon lived in the Abbey at Whitby for the rest of his life. He never became boastful about his songs, for he knew that they were a gift from God.

The Saxon king, Alfred, is often given the name 'the Great'. He is most famous for his struggles to keep the Danes from invading his kingdom of West Sussex. Year after year he gathered his people together and marched to whichever part of the country the Danes were threatening. In the first year of his reign he fought eight battles and countless smaller fights.

But Alfred was not only interested in fighting. He also encouraged poets, artists, teachers and all sorts of learned people to come to his court. At that time, there were very few people who could read and write, so Alfred sent to other kingdoms asking learned and holy men to come and teach the people. One of these was a Welsh monk called Asser. It is clear that Asser became great friends with Alfred, and he wrote the story of King Alfred's life. In Asser's book he tells us many little things that happened when he was with King Alfred, not just the great events of the kingdom. This is one story he told, as he might have told it to a friend in later years.

(*Let the child playing Asser take over the reading.*)

One of King Alfred's greatest sorrows was that he had never learned to read and write as a child. He had a wonderful memory – they tell me that even when he was quite young he would listen to the Saxon poets, and repeat the poems he heard perfectly. And he was one of those people who loved to find things out. If there was a question to which no-one knew the answer, he loved to ponder and puzzle it out.

When I first knew him he was just learning to read and write. It's hard to imagine, isn't it, with all the troubles he had in his kingdom, that he still found time to sit down and struggle with his books. For it was a struggle for him. It's always harder for an adult to learn than a child. He had got to the stage where he could just about make out the words in a book, but he found it very difficult to make any sense of them until someone explained it. That was part of my job, to help him understand the books he wanted to read.

I remember particularly one evening when he and I were sitting together discussing this and that, as we often did. I happened to quote something from a book I had been reading. Alfred went quiet. He was clearly impressed with what I had said, and I could see him thinking it over.

'Tell me that again!' he demanded.

I repeated the quotation slowly and carefully.

'I like that!' he said. 'That's something really important!'

All of a sudden he started wriggling around, and tugging at his cloak. I couldn't work out what he was doing until he pulled out a little book from the folds of his cloak. It was battered and worn, but he handled it almost with love.

'This goes everywhere with me,' he said. 'Look.'

Inside I found written some of the Church's Daily Service, some other prayers and some psalms.

'How did you get this?' I asked.

'I remember hearing those prayers when I was quite small,' he replied. 'I used to say them to myself when times were hard and I had no one to turn to, except God. Then when I began to be able to write things down, I put them into this book, so that I could carry them about with me. Now I want you to write down those words which you just quoted to me, so that I can carry them with me too.'

What a king he was! To be so keen to study and remember God's word, even with all the things he had to do. As I turned the pages of his little book, I gave thanks to God for him.

'Come on! Come on!' broke in Alfred. 'Why aren't you writing it down?'

'Well, the trouble is,' I said, 'there isn't really any room in this book. Would you mind if I wrote it on a separate sheet? Because then, if you come across something else you like, I could write that down with it.'

'That's a wonderful idea!' he said eagerly. 'Do it now, straight away!'

So as quickly as I could, I put together a little book, and wrote down the passage that meant so much to him. From then on, whenever we were talking, the king was always on the watch for more passages he could put in his book. I might quote something from the Bible, and he would ask me to write

that down, or the teachings of the Church Fathers. Day by day the book grew, and we had to add more sheets to it. King Alfred was so happy and busy collecting these words he loved – he reminded me of a bee in summer, going round from flower to flower, gathering nectar first from one, and then from another, and storing up all their sweetness in the cells of his honeycomb. He told me that whenever he found things difficult he would open his book, which he called his 'handbook', and read something in it. It always made him feel better.

And do you know, I think that was the beginning of his own writing and translating work. That handbook came to mean so much to him, he wanted others to know more of the treasures stored up in it. That was what started him translating some of it from Latin into Anglo-Saxon, the language that ordinary people spoke. And of course it didn't stop there. Eventually he was translating whole books of the Bible and writing them down so that his people could understand them. It all started with that little book.

(*Resume the story yourself.*)

Since Alfred's time, many people have done the same. They may collect Bible quotations, or poems, or other things they have read, or things that people have said to them. It doesn't have to be in any special order, it's just anything that they feel is worth remembering.

Time traveller: Well, there's no doubt that I'm in the capital city of a great kingdom. You've only to look round at the busy streets and the new building going on. I'll just ask this person to tell us a little more about this city. (*To passer-by.*) Excuse me, I understand that the present monarch's family have not ruled the country for very long?

Passer-by: Yes, it all started with our great ruler's grandfather, who won the kingdom in battle. But now the country is prosperous. There are merchants going out to trade in all sorts of places, and bringing back precious and beautiful things.

Time traveller: I imagine court life is very sumptuous – all the most important people gathered at the palace?

Passer-by: Yes, our ruler has gathered a lot of very clever and talented people at the court, and if you want to get on in this kingdom, that's the place to be.

Time traveller: What about religion? I gather that has been a problem recently.

Passer-by: That's true, but the government is keen to make sure that it doesn't turn into religious fighting.

Time traveller: But what does the queen herself think about all this?

Passer-by: The queen? I don't think any of the Emperor's wives have much to say in the matter.

Time traveller: What Emperor? I'm talking about the Queen Elizabeth, daughter of Henry VIII, grand-daughter of Henry VII, who won the kingdom in battle!

Passer-by: Never heard of her. I'm talking about the great Emperor Akbar, son of Humayan, grandson of Babur, who won the kingdom in battle. I don't know what remote part of the world your Queen Elizabeth rules, but here in Northern India is where it's all happening as far as I can see.

Narrator: In north-west India, and the area that is Pakistan today, the Mogul Emperor Akbar was at the height of his power at the same time that Queen Elizabeth ruled England. Akbar ruled from 1556 to 1605. Akbar's father died when Akbar was only 13, and Akbar inherited the throne. He was brave – some described him as foolishly headstrong – and enjoyed active pastimes, hunting, riding elephants and fighting. But he also admired learning (although he didn't want to do too much of it himself!) and art.

During his reign, the painting and architecture in his lands were famous. In 1569 Akbar began building a beautiful new city to celebrate the birth of his son. The city was called Fatehpur Sikri, and its magnificent buildings can still be seen today.

In India at that time, religious differences were as deep and as difficult to handle as in England. The Emperor Akbar was a Muslim, and so were many of his people. But most people, including many of the local rulers, were Hindus. Each ruler, in each area, tried to make his subjects follow his faith.

But Akbar wanted to be Emperor not just of the Muslims, but of all religions. He allowed people to follow their own religion, and he abolished a special tax that had been paid by non-Muslims. He was interested in religion, and liked to listen to religious discussions between people of different faiths. When Christians first arrived in India, he invited some of them to tell him about their faith, and to argue with the Muslims. Akbar even tried to start his own religion – a sort of mixture of the faiths he had learned about – but no-one else was interested, and some people were upset by his ideas.

Not everything was good under Akbar's rule – many of the poor people had to pay heavy taxes to maintain the soldiers, scholars and artists that Akbar employed. But his empire flourished, and when, just after his death, the English King James sent his son a present, the new Emperor thought it was very insignificant, and that the English had no civilisation or wealth worth bothering about!

(*If appropriate the Narrator could continue as follows.*)

Thousands of miles from India, and thousands of miles from Britain, another great kingdom was growing in West Africa – the kingdom of Benin. It was ruled by the Oba, who had control over hundreds of local chiefs whom he had conquered in war.

The city of Benin was clearly impressive. It was divided into two, one side being for the Oba and his family and officials. The palace was huge, with reception rooms, living quarters, and storerooms. Visitors described it as being covered in polished copper, with designs carved on it. The rest of the town was also impressive: there were chief's houses, and whole streets devoted to the different trades of a large city – doctors, hunters, carvers, etc.

The Oba lived in great state, and was hardly ever seen, even by his chiefs. They had to wait to be invited into his presence, and even then they could not speak directly to him, but only through a messenger. Once a year the Oba made a procession through the streets with his hundreds of wives and his palace officials in special ceremonial clothes.

During the sixteenth century there were four great Obas who increased the size of the kingdom by making war on their neighbours. They were very interested in the contacts that were beginning to be made with Europe, and one of them, Esigie, was very friendly towards the Portuguese, and welcomed Christian missionaries to his court.

(The Leader enters holding the 'Bible'. He goes to walk past the woman teacher, but she stops him.)

Teacher: What's that you've got there?

Leader: It's the new edition of the Bible, the one that's in all the churches in England.

Teacher: Oh, I see. Well, it's no good me looking at it then. It'll be in Latin, like all church Bibles.

Leader: No, this one's in English. Just recently, in 1538, it was ordered that every church should have a Bible in English. The translation was done by Miles Coverdale.

Teacher: Oh, then I could have a look at it and understand it. May I? *(She holds out her hand.)*

Leader: Well, no, it isn't quite that simple. Since then people have begun to wonder about letting just anyone read the Bible. People can get some funny ideas after reading the Bible. Most people ought to have someone to explain it to them and make sure they don't get the wrong idea. There's a law just been passed, in 1543, that lays down who can read it. Are you of noble birth?

Teacher: Well, no, I'm not. But I'm quite well educated!

Leader: Doesn't make any difference. You're not even a member of the landed gentry? *(The Teacher shakes her head.)* No? I'm sorry I can't let you read it. The law's the law.

(A Merchant (male) enters.)

Merchant: What's this? The Bible? May I have a look?

Leader: Yes, here you are, you can read it if you like.

Teacher: Wait a minute! You're not a nobleman are you?

Merchant: No, I'm just a wool-merchant. But I had some schooling. I can read English. I'm not brilliant at Latin, mind you.

Teacher (to Leader): Why can he read it and I can't? I thought you said only the gentry and nobility were allowed?

Leader: Well, he's a man, isn't he, and a merchant. We wouldn't let any of the common people read it, the labourers and so on. But a merchant can read it. Mind you *(turns to Merchant)*, don't you go reading it aloud at home. And don't let your wife and daughters read it themselves – that's not allowed.

(A Noblewoman enters.)

Teacher: Well, what about her? She's obviously a noblewoman. You would have let me look at it if I had said I was a member of the nobility. Can she read the Bible?

Leader: Well, yes, she can. *(He goes to give the Bible to the Noblewoman, but then hesitates and takes it back.)* But only in private, mind! You're not to read it aloud, your ladyship. If you want someone to read the Bible to the rest of your household and your family, you'll have to get your husband to do that.

Teacher: So, let me get this straight. A humble person below the rank of merchant can't read the Bible at all. They'd have to go to church to hear it. A merchant can read the Bible himself, but can't read it aloud to anyone else. And even if his wife and daughters are well-educated, they're not allowed to read it at all. Members of the nobility and gentry can read it in private whether they're men or women, but only men are allowed to read it to other people.

Leader: That's right, that's what the law says.

Narrator: In the centre of Manchester stands a large stone monument. On it are carved parts of a letter from Abraham Lincoln, the great President of the USA whose fight against slavery led the USA into a terrible civil war from 1861 to 1864. But why should Abraham Lincoln have written to the people of Manchester and Lancashire?

In the middle of the nineteenth century, Lancashire and Manchester were the main places in the world where cotton was spun. Every day the noise of the cotton machines rang out as workers spun the cotton and turned it into cloth which was then sold all around the world.

Much of this cotton was picked in the cotton fields of the Southern States of the USA and then shipped to the mills in Lancashire. But the cotton was not picked by men and women who were paid for their work; it was picked by slaves, men, women and children who had been taken prisoner in their homeland of Africa and transported to the United States. These slaves often lived in terrible conditions, but above all they had no freedom, bought and sold at the whim of their masters.

When Abraham Lincoln became President of the USA in 1860, he declared that the slavery in the Southern States must end. The white men in the Southern States did not want the Northern States telling them what to do. They wanted to keep their slaves, so they broke away from the Northern States declaring that they wouldn't be part of the United States any more. War would follow immediately.

When the Civil War began, Lincoln ordered that all the Southern States which still had slavery should be blockaded. This meant that the Southern States could not send their goods like cotton overseas. This blockade affected the cotton mills of Lancashire very badly. The workers in the mills were dependent on this cotton coming or they would have little or no work. No work would mean no job; no job meant no money; no money meant nothing to buy food with.

It looked to many as if the British Government would give in and import cotton from the Southern States, but the cotton workers would not. Even though it meant less work and so less money, they refused to touch any cotton from the rebel Southern States. More than this, they raised money to send to help the fight against slavery.

On 31st December 1862:
A child (reading from a mock-up of the 'Morning Star' newspaper): A large and enthusiastic meeting was held in the Free Trade Hall, Manchester, on Wednesday evening, which had been called by a committee of working men, to let the working classes of Manchester and Salford express their sympathy with the North in America, and to pass resolutions in support of President Lincoln's policy of freeing the slaves.

There were many well-known people on the platform, including Mr Jackson, who had been a slave owned by the Southern President Jefferson Davis, but who had escaped. There were several speeches by the workers.
Second child: I have come here because I believe that the interests of the working people – that the interests, in

fact, of this great country – are closely bound up with the question we are discussing tonight.

(*Cries of 'Hear, Hear!'*)

Third child: There have been articles in some newspapers suggesting that we in Britain ought to support the South, so that we can get cotton. Many of our leaders in England want to support the Southern States. The magazine 'Punch' even had a poem about it:

Though with the North we sympathize,
It must not be forgotten,
That with the South we've stronger ties,
Which are composed of cotton.

Some people are trying to tell us that the war is not about slavery at all, but about whether one state can tell another what to do. They say that the South is fighting for freedom. But I say that it is not freedom to sell human beings like household goods.

(*Applause*)

Fourth child: I have no doubt that the only thing the Southern States want is to go on owning slaves, and that that is the only reason they are fighting. I pray that they will fail in this horrible purpose. I hope that this meeting will be the first of many throughout this country.

Fifth child: If one person has a right to improve his mind, and to do his best to rise in the world, then so do the slaves in the Southern States of America.

Sixth child: Certain people have said, 'We need cotton. Let's support the Southern States, and we shall get it.' After they've eaten their beef and plum-pudding, with their wine in front of them, that is easy to say. But the working people of England are prepared to keep their dignity. This war should not end in a way that makes slavery permanent. 'Onward, you free men of the north,' and 'Downward, you southern men who want slavery!'

(*Applause*)

Seventh child: Friends, let me propose a resolution: 'that this meeting, recognising the sacred right of every human being to personal freedom and protection under the law, expresses its detestation of black slavery in America.

All: Yes! Yes! The resolution is carried!

Narrator: Then someone suggested that they should send a letter to President Lincoln to tell him of their support. This, too, was agreed, and the letter sent. Abraham Lincoln immediately wrote back to thank them.

Eighth child: 'I know and deeply deplore the sufferings which the working people of Manchester and all Europe are called to endure in this crisis.... It is indeed a reinspiring assurance of the... ultimate and universal triumph of justice, humanity and freedom.'

Narrator: After three and a half years the war finished. The Northern States had won and slavery was abolished. The English workers had had to suffer hardship while they supported the ban on Southern States cotton, but this suffering had helped to win the war and win freedom for thousands of slaves. That is why, in the centre of Manchester to this day, you will find words from Lincoln's letter carved in stone and set in a place of honour.

In 1853, Great Britain went to war against Russia in a place called the Crimea. It was a terrible war; pointless, bloody and badly organised. This had been the same with many of the wars Great Britain had fought for hundreds of years. However, the Crimean War was different. *The Times* newspaper had a journalist at the war. His name was William Howard Russell. There had never been a journalist officially at a war before. From the front line he sent back long reports on the progress, or rather the failure, of the war. He reported all the stupid actions of those in charge of the war, and the anger of the ordinary soldiers.

For example, one of his reports was about boots sent to the soldiers. It was getting bitterly cold in the Crimean winter and all the soldiers had were ordinary shoes. So large numbers of boots were packaged up and shipped out to the Crimea. But when the tens of thousands of boots arrived, the soldiers discovered that they were all left foot boots – no right foot boots to pair up with them! Stupid things like this had happened in previous wars but no one had been there to report them. Now all the British public could read about it.

Russell also reported on the terrible living conditions of the soldiers. He wrote about the poor food they were given, the thin tents they lived in and the way their officers seemed to ignore them. He wrote about the great bravery of many of the soldiers in battle, but his reports also expressed his anger at the fact some generals didn't seem to know what to do.

When people in Great Britain read these stories in *The Times*, they began to ask questions about the way soldiers were cared for and the way the war was being run. They began to see that war was not just a question of who won. People began to want to know why Great Britain was at war and what we might win at the end. They wanted to know why the war was being run so badly and how to help the soldiers. These questions made life very difficult for the Government but helped to make life a little better for the soldiers as the war dragged on until 1856.

Russell's reporting also helped Florence Nightingale, a woman who volunteered to nurse the wounded soldiers. She too was appalled at the lack of hygiene and the terrible conditions. She bullied the generals into improving the conditions in the hospital tents.

Ever since Russell's reports, journalists have tried to cover wars so that people at home could know what was really going on. They report on the bravery and sometimes the success, but they also report on the pain, bloodshed, mistakes and mismanagement.

Imagine what it must be like to go to bed at night wondering whether there will be the screeching sounds of air-raid sirens, piercing your sleep, summoning you to go underground to the shelters below. That is what it was like for people for much of the Second World War in many parts of Britain. But for the people of Coventry the night of Thursday, 14th November, 1942, was the most terrible of all nights in the Second World War. German planes had swept over the city, dropping bomb after bomb after bomb, leaving a trail of destruction in their flight path.

The next morning the people of Coventry wept for their dead. Many were now also homeless. It was a time of grief and despair. It was a time of anger towards those who had killed their loved ones and destroyed their city. Many were angry not only at the pilots who had dropped the bombs, and the men who had commanded them, but towards all Germans.

In the heart of Coventry the great cathedral had also been hit by bombs. For many hundreds of years it had towered over the city, now like so many of the buildings around it, it too was in ruins with only the walls left standing.

The cathedral caretaker, Jock Forbes went to inspect the damage. As he stood among the rubble he thought of another day long, long before, another day of despair and grief. He thought of Jesus dying on the cross while his mother and friends wept nearby. He thought of the way Jesus said, 'Father, forgive them' about his enemies, even though he was suffering so much pain. He thought too, of the Christian belief

that Jesus rose from the dead, giving hope that good can come out of evil, that life can begin again after a time of grief. The cross of Jesus was a symbol of all the suffering in the world, but also of hope and forgiveness.

Jock hoped that his fellow citizens in Coventry would look to the future and learn to forgive the Germans. He took two charred beams that had once been part of the old cathedral roof and made them into a cross. He stuck the cross into an old dustbin filled with earth, so that anyone coming to the cathedral would see it.

The wooden cross, standing in the cathedral grounds, became a symbol of hope and forgiveness for the people of Coventry in those sad days. They gradually rebuilt their homes and their lives and, next to the ruins of the old cathedral, a new cathedral was built.

The new cathedral is a modern cathedral. It symbolises hope for the future, hope for a world in which all people live in peace together, forgiving each other. The staff at the cathedral and many of those who worship there, work for peace. They have made friends and shared activities with Germans, especially those who live in the city of Dresden which was heavily bombed by British aeroplanes during the Second World War.

In the ruins of the old cathedral a small chapel had been made and in it stands the cross of charred beams. Behind the cross are the words 'Father Forgive'. In front is another cross made from thick fourteenth century nails from the old cathedral roof. Together the two crosses stand as a symbol of hope and forgiveness.

Sometimes it isn't easy to find the money to pay for a new church. This is the story of how one vicar solved the problem.

In 1904, the village of Biggin Hill, in Kent, had a population of about 200 people. They had no church building, so the people built a small iron hut, which they thought would do for a few years until they could afford to build a proper church. By 1951, however, the population had grown to nearly 4,000, but the tiny iron building was still the only church. The people had tried hard to save enough money to build a new church, but it seemed that as soon as the money was saved, the price of a building had gone up again!

Then a new vicar called Vivian Symons came to the village. He looked at the tiny, shabby church, and said, 'This will not do! God deserves a better church than this!'

But there was still not enough money. Then the vicar had an idea.

'In London there are churches that nobody uses any more,' he said. 'The people have moved to different places to live, and the church buildings are empty. Why don't we ask to take down one of these churches and build it again here in Biggin Hill?'

'But who will do all the work?' the people asked.

'We will!' he replied. 'With God's help.'

Many people laughed at the idea, but Vivian Symons did not give up. He found a disused church and got permission to move it. Then, in the middle of a London street, he faced the church and said in a loud voice, 'In the name of Jesus Christ, be removed to the Parish of Biggin Hill!'

Then the hard work started. He knew that the church would not move by itself. But he believed that God was helping him and his congregation to move it. When anything was needed, a lorry or some scaffolding, for example, he would go to the building firms and say to them, 'God needs to borrow some scaffolding – will you lend me yours?' And they did.

For over three years the vicar and the congregation worked at taking down the old church and moving the bricks, stones and wood to Biggin Hill. Many people gave money to help, and one gave a piece of land where the new church could be built. The people worked at clearing and levelling the land. Finally, six years after they had started, everything was ready to start the new building. Vivian Symons was quite willing to do this himself if necessary, but a local firm of builders offered to do the job without making any money out of it. While they worked, the congregation made many beautiful things for the inside of the church.

The church was finished in 1959, and the bells rang out for the first time to celebrate. To many of the congregation, their new church building was all the more precious because they had done so much of the work themselves.

Muslims believe the Angel Gabriel came from God and taught Muhammad about how people should live in obedience to God. The words that the Angel Gabriel taught Muhammad were written down and became the book, the Qur'an. Today all over the world there are many millions of people who try to live by the teachings in the Qur'an. They meet together in buildings called mosques. Some of the mosques were built hundreds of years ago, while others were built quite recently. Sometimes there is not enough money or the land available to build a new mosque. So Muslims turn a house or a warehouse or sometimes a church which Christians no longer use into a mosque. This story, though, is about the building of the very first mosque.

When Muhammad first told Allah's message in Makkah, only a few people believed him. Many thought he was lying or mad. Muhammad preached in the market-place and told the traders not to cheat their customers. The traders hated him for upsetting their businesses and soon started attacking his followers. Some messengers came from Medina and invited Muhammad and his followers to come and live in their city where they would be safe. The Muslims accepted and set out to Medina. This journey is known as the Hijrah and the year it took place became Year 1 in the Muslim calendar.

When Muhammad arrived in Medina, the people welcomed him and everyone wanted him to go and live in their house. If Muhammad had agreed to live with one family he would have offended all the others. So he let his camel, Qaswah, wander through the streets. Eventually she lay down in an open space near some palm trees. Muhammad bought this piece of land and built a simple house with a large courtyard. This place became the first mosque where Muslims would come to pray.

The whistling wind
O wind, why do you never rest
Wandering, whistling to and fro
Bringing rain out of the west
From the dim north bringing snow.

Christina Rossetti

The wind
Who has seen the wind?
Neither I nor you:
But when the leaves hang trembling
The wind is passing through.

Who has seen the wind?
Neither you or I:
But when the trees bow down their heads
The wind is passing by.

Christina Rossetti

Windy nights

Whenever the moon and stars are set,
Whenever the wind is high,
All night long in the dark and wet,
A man goes riding by.
Late in the night when the fires are out,
Why does he gallop and gallop about?

Whenever the trees are crying aloud,
And the ships are tossed at sea,
By, on the highway, low and loud,
By at the gallop goes he:
By at the gallop he goes, and then
By he comes at the gallop again.

Robert Louis Stevenson

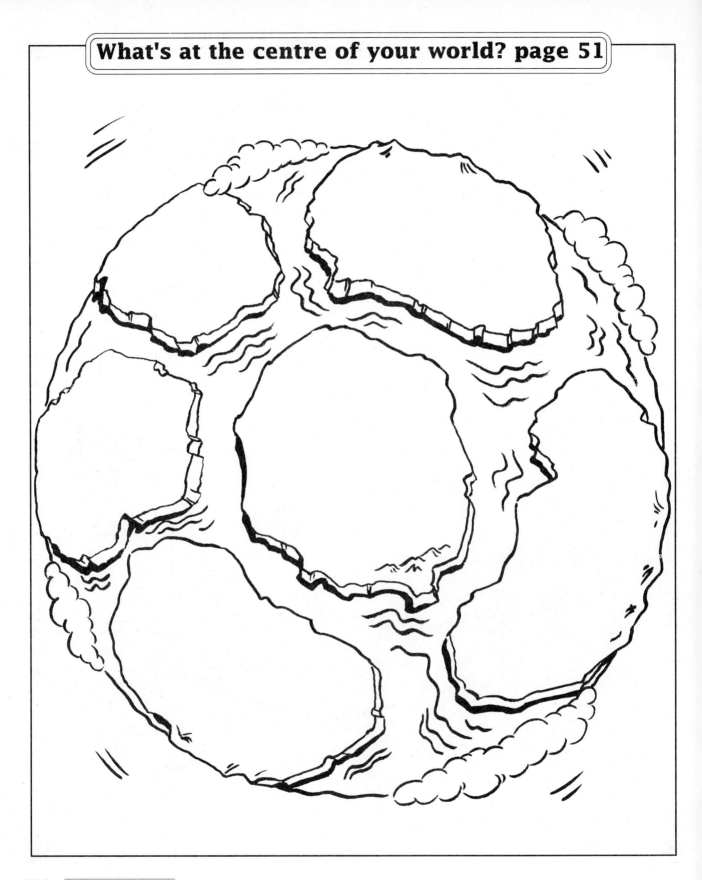

Imagine you are going to a place where you really like being, where you have felt happy and have enjoyed being before. Perhaps it is somewhere very close, a corner of your own home or school, or perhaps it is far away and you have to travel to get there. Can you see some of the colours around you? Is there just one colour you remember or are they all jumbled up? Imagine the sounds around you, of the people there. Or perhaps there are animals, or faint sounds of other things in the distance. Or perhaps there is no sound. Can you smell anything that makes you feel happy? Is there anything that you want to touch in the place you are visiting?

Footsteps map, pages 54 & 55

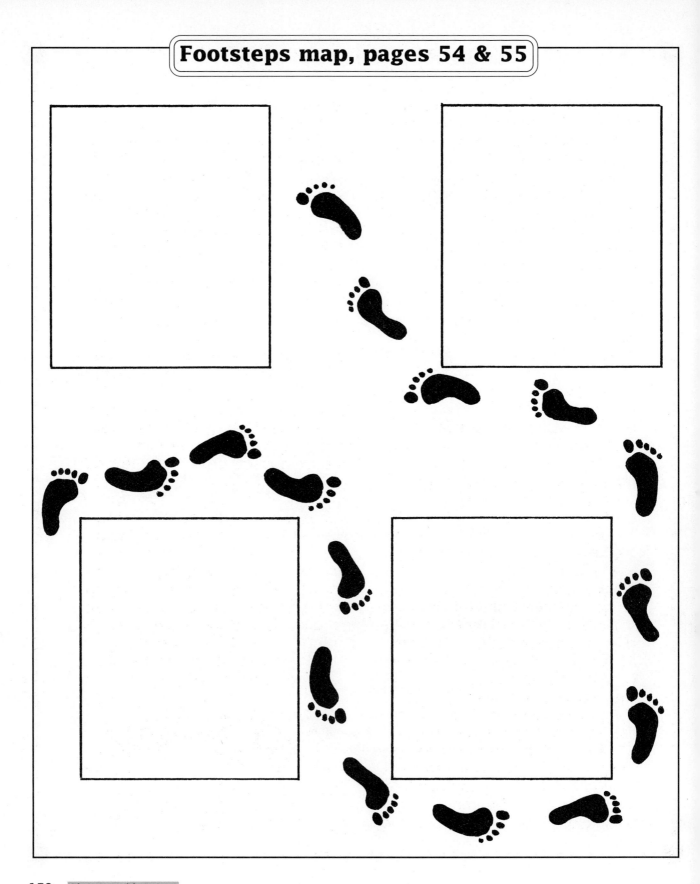

When the first English people went to Australia, they thought that the land didn't belong to anyone. They couldn't see any fences or walls and there were no land deeds, so they said to themselves, 'This land doesn't belong to anyone, so we'll claim it for the King of England.' So they put a flag up and said, 'This land belongs to the King of England.' Then they put up walls and fences.

First of all they used the land as a place for prisoners whom they had brought from England, because there was no room in the prisons in England. Then they started giving away the land – to the soldiers who came to guard the prisoners, to the prisoners who had finished their sentences and didn't want to go back to England, and then later to free people who wanted to go to Australia to farm or make a new home.

Sometimes when the British people ventured further away from the new towns and into the bush, they would clear away the bush and put up fences, and write and ask permission to settle on the land. They would be given the deeds to the land to show it belonged to them. Later still, the Government sold the land to people who wanted it and these people were also given land deeds to show that the land belonged to them.

The king, the governor, the soldiers, the convicts and the free settlers all thought the land was empty before the white men came. They thought that it didn't belong to anyone. They thought they could do what they liked with it.

But the trouble was that the land did belong to someone, or rather it sort of did. The land was not a big empty space with nothing in it. There were people and there were animals. There were people who had lived in Australia for thousands of years, people called native Australians, or Australian Aboriginals. There were lots of animals, such as koalas, kangaroos and wombats.

There was a big difference between the British settlers and the Australian Aboriginals in their attitude to land. The British settlers thought you could own land and you could buy and sell it or give it away if you wanted to. But the Australian Aboriginals thought that all the land belonged to everybody and every creature who lived on it, so they didn't build fences round it and say, 'This bit belongs to me' and 'This bit belongs to him'. In a way, it was as though the people belonged to the land rather than the land belonging to the people. Just as you belong to a family, but you don't own the family, so the Aboriginal people thought they belonged to the land but they didn't own it.

A valuable mineral called uranium is found under the ground in Northern Australia. When it was discovered there, the mining companies went to the Australian government and told them that they would pay a lot of money for the right to dig up the land and dig out the uranium. The Australian government was glad to be able to earn the money.

But then there were protests. The first Australians, the Aboriginals, who had lived in Australia for thousands of years, said, 'You can't do this because this land doesn't belong to you. It belongs to the Aboriginal tribes.'

And they said, 'You can't dig this up because this land is our sacred space. It is the land where we go to have our secret ceremonies. These are the dreamtime places. Long ago our dreamtime ancestors came out of the land. They showed us how to make fire. They showed us how to fish. They showed us where the best berries grow. They showed us how to find water in the desert. And where they walked and talked and showed us these things is very important. These are sacred places, they have been sacred places for thousands of years. You shall not dig them up for some metal and spoil them. They are valuable to you because they seem to contain a great treasure which will make you much money. They are valuable to us because they are our sacred sites.' The government, the mining companies and the Aboriginals argued for many years. They went to court and they protested on the street. In the end, the Aboriginals won the right of ownership for some of the land.

But the story isn't quite finished. Many of the Aboriginals want to keep the land as sacred sites, as a place to hold their ceremonies and as a place to remember the dreamtime ancestors. But some Aboriginals, just a few, want to sell the mining rights to the mining company. They say it would make lots of money to make life easier for the Aboriginal people.

And all the time the mining companies are finding new seams of uranium and other valuable minerals, and all the time the Aboriginals are having to continue to fight for more of their land.

Imagine you are riding in a jeep. It is a very bumpy journey as there is no proper road. Out of the window, all you can see is flat land stretching on for miles and miles and miles. There is some yellow, dry grass but mostly the land is brown and red because you are in the middle of the great stony desert in central Australia. Suddenly on the horizon you can see what looks like a great rocky hill, looming up towards you. It is like a hill but its sides look very steep. There are little holes in the side, at least that's what they appear to be at first, but when you get closer you can see they are caves.

(*Ask the children to open their eyes and then continue.*)

The rock you have been imagining has two names. The white Australians call it Ayers Rock, but the first Australians, the Aboriginal people, have a much older name for it, a name they have called it for thousands of years. They call in Uluru. From sunrise to sunset Uluru changes in colour, as the sun moves across the sky and casts shadows upon it. It changes from orange to red to purple over the course of the day. All over it are small water holes, because beneath it there is underground water.

Uluru is a mysterious place. Sometimes it can feel quite frightening to be on the rock or to stand beneath it and watch it tower overhead. The Aboriginals say that it grew from a tiny sandhill during the time of creation, in the 'dreamtime'. They say that this is one of the places from where the dreamtime ancestors came to shape the world and teach the Aboriginals the wisdom of the land.

Lots of tourists like to visit Uluru or Ayers Rock as they call it. They enjoy its great beauty, but many of them have not treated it properly. Many of them have treated it as just a great big outcrop of rock rather than something to be looked after and cared for. They have scrambled all over the rock, they have broken branches, they have taken home pieces of the rock as souvenirs. They have left litter over it. It grieved the Aboriginal people to see their holy place suffer and they wept.

In 1985, the Australian government gave Uluru back to the Aboriginal people so they could guard it. The tourists still come to the rock, but the descendants of the white settlers are learning to call it by its ancient name and are learning to treat it with respect.

Running through Uluru is a deep gorge. Boulders lie scattered about this gorge and at the head are tall slabs of rocks. There are lots of small tufts of grass dotted about the gorge and there is a deep hole. Scientists can give an explanation for how the gorge came about and why there are strewn boulders, but the Aboriginal people tell another tale.

They say that way back in the dreamtime when the land was still forming, the snake people travelled across the dry desert land from water hole to water hole. At last they made camp on a long, low sandhill and there they lived happily and peacefully for many years. Every day the men went out hunting and every day they returned at sunset and rested on the edge of the sandhill. Every day the women gathered food in their straw baskets and baked bread from the grass seeds. Eventually the time came for them to return to the earth from which they had come. As they did so the sandhill turned into a huge rock. The women became the boulders in the gorge, their straw baskets became the tall slabs of rock. Their hair turned into the small tufts of grass and the camp-fire where they had been baking their bread turned into the deep hole.

As for the men lying resting on the side of the sandhill, they turned into boulders which you can still see today on the flat plains beneath the great rock.

When the Aboriginal people visit the rock, they think of the stories of the dreamtime and of the snake people.

The Aboriginal people are not the only ones to tell stories about how the land became different shapes, about why there are mountains and rivers in certain places and why lakes look as they do. People from all round the world have told stories like that. It helps them think of the time before time when all was being created.

The bird and the crumb

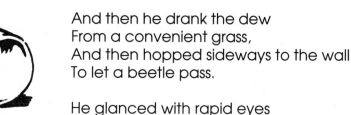

A bird came down the walk:
He did not know I saw;
He bit an angle-worm in halves
And ate the fellow, raw.

And then he drank the dew
From a convenient grass,
And then hopped sideways to the wall
To let a beetle pass.

He glanced with rapid eyes
That hurried all abroad,
They looked like frightened beads, I thought.
He stirred his velvet head

Like one in danger; cautious,
I offered him a crumb,
And he unrolled his feathers
And rowed him softer home

Than oars divide the ocean,
Too silver for a seam,
Or butterflies, off banks of noon,
Leap, splashless, as they swim.

Emily Dickinson

The African elephant is much larger than the Indian elephant and can't be domesticated or tamed as the Indian elephant can. The Indian elephant can be trained to carry people on its back. Not so long ago in Great Britain you could have a ride on an elephant in the zoo, and Indian elephants also did tricks in circuses. But the African elephant is not like that. It is bigger, and wilder, than the Indian elephant. African elephants live in herds and when they are moving fast, thundering through the jungle or across clearings, everything and everybody is in danger. Often the elephants tear down fences and trample crops.

But although the elephant can be a dangerous animal, it is the elephant itself which is in danger. Sometimes in the African bush you come across a baby elephant standing piteously by the dead body of its mother. Usually hunters have killed the mother because her tusks are very valuable as they are made of ivory, and ivory can be carved into beautiful ornaments. The hunters take away the tusks and sell them secretly.

It is not just that individual elephants are in danger, there is the danger that the whole population of elephants will be wiped out.

The trouble is that when the hunters look at the elephant, they don't think about an animal who is enjoying life. They don't think about an animal who has young or parents and companions. The hunters just look at the elephant and think *money*.

Neither do the hunters think about the fact that if the killing continues there will be no more elephants left.

The Bible and the Qur'an teach that people should take care of the natural world. They can use it, but not destroy it. These hunters are failing to take care of the world.

But there are people who are working to try to protect the elephants. The governments of some African countries put elephant hunters in prison if they can catch them, and make game parks and wildlife sanctuaries, where the elephants can live in peace and safety. And there are charities like the Worldwide Fund for Nature who are helping the governments.

Robert Bruce was a king of Scotland in the days when Scotland was an independent country. The English often invaded Scotland and took over parts of it, and Robert Bruce led his soldiers time and time against the English soldiers to try to drive them out of his country, but he was always beaten. One day, exhausted from battle, he took shelter in a cave with a few soldiers. He sat down in despair.

'I shall never be able to free my country from the English!' he said to himself. 'I might as well give up. Every time I try, it ends in disaster.'

But as he sat there brooding, thinking of how his people would suffer if he gave up, he noticed a movement near him in the cave. A spider was trying to build a web across a corner of the cave. The spider first had to make a line of silk, and then swing across the gap to fasten the line the other side. Time after time the spider spun a thin line, and tried to swing across. But every time it tried, the silk broke and the spider fell to the ground. 'Poor spider,' said Robert. 'You're like me, trying and trying but failing every time. You'll give up too, in the end. Nothing and no one can go on and on when everything goes wrong.'

So he watched to see how many times the spider would try. And he watched. And he watched. But the spider never gave up. It went on and on patiently spinning its silk and trying to get across the gap to start its web. Robert lost count of the number of times that spider fell down and started again. Then, at long last, the spider managed to swing across, fasten its silken line, and begin making a beautiful web.

'It did it!' cried Robert. 'It went on and on, and finally it succeeded. If a tiny spider can go on like that and finally achieve what it set out to do, then why am I giving up? I'll settle down right now to think what my next plan will be to beat the English invaders!'

Why is it that snakes slide on their bellies across the earth and do not have legs like other land creatures? The scientists tell one story, the Bible tells another.

Long ago, when the world was very new, the first man, Adam, and the first woman, Eve, lived in a garden that God had made for them. Now God had said to them, 'You may eat the fruit from any of the trees in the garden but one. You must not eat the fruit of the tree of the knowledge of good and evil.'

For a while the first man and the first woman were content and enjoyed the fruit of all the other trees and did not even touch the tree of knowledge of good and evil.

Then one day, as Eve was lingering near the forbidden tree, the snake, that most deceitful of all creatures, poked his head round the tree and said to her, 'Did God really say you mustn't eat any of the fruit from the garden?'

The woman replied, 'We can eat the fruit of any of the trees in the garden, but we must not eat the fruit of the tree in the middle of the garden or we shall die.'

'No,' said the snake. 'Don't be fooled. You will not die. God doesn't want you to eat of that tree because that is the tree of the knowledge of good and evil. God is jealous. He doesn't want you to become like Him.'

Eve listened to the snake's words and looked longingly at the fruit of the forbidden tree. She saw how delicious its fruit would be to eat and she wanted, oh how she wanted, the knowledge it would bring. So she reached out and picked some of the fruit and tasted it and then she gave some to her husband to eat.

What happened?

The first man and the first woman looked at each other and for the first time knew that they were naked and they were embarrassed. So they covered themselves with leaves from a fig tree. They could no longer live forever contentedly in that garden but had to leave it, banished to the world outside the garden where there was decay and death.

As for the snake, God said to it, 'You are cursed more than any other creature. You will crawl on your belly and eat the dust of the earth. You and the woman will always be enemies; your children and her children will always be enemies. You will bite their heels and they will crush you with their feet.'

Other cultures have stories about the snake playing an important role right back at the beginning of all things. Many also describe the snake as a most terrifying, but also a very clever, creature. One such group of people are the Yanomamo Indians who live far away in the Amazonian jungle of South America. For many centuries they have lived among trees and the creepers, with the monkeys and jaguars, the great croaking frogs, the multi-coloured birds, and many other creatures in the sweltering hot climate. It is a hard place to live but they have survived, taking only what they need from the jungle, finding food in various secret places that no outsider could ever find and learning how to plant seeds that will help the jungle grow. They have learned too which plants will help cure illnesses. And all the while the jungle has flourished and has continued to feed them.

So how did they learn the secrets of the jungle so that they could live in it in such a harmonious way?

According to the Yanomamo, their ancestors learned these secrets long ago from the giant anaconda snake who was wise beyond wise. It was he who taught them all they needed to know to live in the jungle.

The giant anaconda snake also taught them to be terrified of him and of the jungle creatures. He taught the Yanomamo to take only what they needed and to live in a way that does not destroy the jungle. He taught them that if they destroyed the jungle they would also destroy themselves.

So the Yanomamo Indians treat the giant anaconda snakes with respect. They honour them for their wisdom and are terrified of them at the same time.

In recent times, city dwellers and woodmen have come to the jungle. They do not treat the anaconda snakes with such respect, but kill them if they can. Nor do they treat the jungle with the respect that the Yanomamo Indians have done. These new people have chopped down the trees so that they can use the wood and they have sent in bulldozers to clear away the jungle so that cattle can graze there. It could take hundreds of years for the jungle to regrow and in the meantime many different species of wildlife are being wiped out and will probably never return.

The people of the jungle, the Yanomamo, are being forced out of the jungle and into the shanty towns on the edges of cities. There they find it hard to get work and find enough to eat. They catch diseases easily and live a poor life.

The teachings about living at peace with the jungle are being ignored, the teachings which the Yanomamo say the great anaconda snake taught them.

Can we learn from animals? According to a Jewish book called the Talmud we can. It says that God teaches us how we ought to behave through the behaviour of animals. The Talmud was written a very long time ago. Its authors had a different understanding of animals compared to many scientists today, so some of the examples it gives seem quite strange. Here are some of them.

• The cat – the Talmud says that the cat shows us that we should be clean in our toilet habits because whenever the cat goes to the toilet it buries its droppings and covers them up.

• The grasshopper – the Talmud says that the grasshopper sings all summer long until its belly bursts and it dies. The Talmud praises the grasshopper because even though it knows what is going to happen, it goes on

singing. It shows us that we should do our duty to God, no matter what the consequences.

• The stork – this bird should be observed carefully because there are two things we can learn from it. First, that it guards its family zealously, protecting them from harm, and second, that it is always compassionate towards its fellow creatures. So we should look after our family but always be kind to others.

• The ant – ants always respect the property of others and never go on territory other than their own. People should do the same.

These observations of animal behaviour were made 1600 years ago and we might not understand or agree with all of them, but today people still praise the way animals behave. They say, 'brave as a lion', 'busy as a bee' or 'wise as an owl'. Maybe there are some things we can learn from animals.

Muhammad and his companions were making camp in the desert. It was a cold night – for the desert can grow very cold when the sun has gone down – and one man had lit a fire. Muhammad was going round the camp checking that everything was all right. All seemed peaceful and he stopped to watch some ants on an ant-hill. They were scurrying backwards and forwards and working hard as ants do. Suddenly Muhammad saw that some of the ants were heading straight for the fire without realising the danger they were in.

'Who made this fire?' he asked.

'I did, O messenger of Allah,' replied the man crouching beside it. 'I was so cold so I made it to keep warm.'

'Quick! Put out the fire. Put out the fire!' ordered the Prophet.

The man obeyed. He didn't know what had gone wrong.

'What's the matter with lighting a fire?' he said to himself. 'I suppose the Prophet knows what he is doing.'

Then he saw the ants and he realised that the fire would have hurt them. He saw that the Prophet had been concerned for the safety of the ants and that's why he ordered that the fire be extinguished. From that day, the man and Muhammad's other companions always looked around first to check that no animals were in danger before lighting a fire.

There are many other stories about Muhammad's compassion for animals. He did eat meat, and Muslims do kill animals for food. But they say they you should only kill animals when it is necessary, and you should take care not to kill or harm them otherwise.

Once when Jesus was talking to a crowd of people, someone came and nudged him. 'Your mother and brothers are waiting for you outside. They are growing impatient.' Jesus looked around him at all the faces, eager to hear his talk about God's kingdom, eager to feel his healing touch.

'These are my brothers and sisters,' he said.

Jesus saw all humanity as his family. They were all related to him and he loved and cared for them.

1200 years after Jesus, there lived in Italy a man called Francis. Francis loved Jesus and tried to be as much like Jesus as he could. He followed the teachings of Jesus because he too believed that his family was not just his own small family, his mother, father and their children. He thought of everyone as his brothers and sisters. But Francis did not stop there. He looked round at the birds and the animals, the sun and the moon, the rain and the wind.

'God made all these, and God made me,' he thought. 'God loves all of these, and God loves me. That must mean that all of these are my brothers and sisters. I should love them like my own family.'

He tried to treat everything and everyone as his brothers and sisters. He did his best to understand what other creatures needed and why they acted as they did.

Once this love of all creatures brought Francis face to face with a wolf. This wolf lived in the hills round the Italian town of Gubbio. He skulked in the woods waiting to pounce on passers-by and kill them. The townspeople were terrified and were too frightened to go out of the town. Francis saw that something must be done. So he walked out into the hills calling to the wolf. Soon they stood opposite each other.

The wolf stood still, shocked to find a person who was not afraid of him, but who looked at him lovingly. Francis lectured the wolf. He told him very sternly that he ought to be kind to his fellow creatures and not hurt them. That he should not kill them.

Then Francis realised that the wolf killed not because he was wicked or evil but because he was hungry. He was not a big bad wolf, but a creature needing food as all creatures need food. So Francis told the wolf he would find him food.

Francis returned to the town and told the people what he had learned. He told them to prepare sacks of food to take to the wolf. At first they were afraid, but they knew that Francis understood wild animals, so they trusted him. From that day on, the townspeople gave the wolf food, and the wolf no longer attacked the people.

Imagine that you are in the most beautiful park you have ever seen. A river bubbles and swirls its way through the garden, fish leaping in its waters. Everywhere there is an abundance of flowers, and their sweet smell surrounds you. Trees shade you from the sun; trees which are laden with all sorts of delicious juicy fruit; apricots, peaches, oranges and many others. Brightly coloured birds sing in the branches and deer come to eat out of your hand. A gentle breeze dances round your face. Everything is perfect.
(*Ask the children to open their eyes and then continue.*)

The Bible says that in the beginning, the first man, Adam, and the first woman, Eve, lived in a perfect place like that. The Jewish faith has many stories about that beginning time, stories which are not found in the Bible but which may help us to understand it. The following is one of them.

On the first day, Adam was walking in the garden, enjoying the breeze when he saw dangling before him a delicious-looking, succulent apricot, and he felt hungry. He thought to himself, 'God said we could eat the fruit of any tree in the garden but the fruit of the tree of knowledge of good and evil. This fruit is not from that tree so I may eat it.'

He stretched out his hand to pluck the fruit, but to his surprise the branch lifted itself out of reach. Adam was puzzled. Every time he tried, the same thing happened.

Then a voice spoke, 'First you must care for the tree, then you may eat fruit from it,' and Adam knew that first he had to look after the trees, then he would be able to enjoy their fruits.

Still today, gardeners and farmers know that if you want to enjoy the pleasures of trees then you have to be able to take care of them.

Much of the land in north-west India is barren and dry. The wind swirls the dust round in the heat, and very little grows. But it was not always like this. Once this was covered with woodlands, but the woods have been chopped down. People have cleared the land to graze their cattle and to grow crops and used the wood for firewood. All the goodness has been taken out of the soil.

But there are a few pockets of land where this is not so and the land is still fertile and things still grow. One of these areas is where the Bishnoi people live.

The Bishnoi are known as 'the people who love trees', and they don't just show their love by watering them, taking care of them or by standing round saying, 'Aren't those trees lovely'. Once the Bishnoi people showed their love for their trees by giving up their lives for them. It happened like this.

200 years ago the Bishnoi were living peacefully on their land. They farmed the land according to the rules their religious teacher, a Hindu called Jumba Ji Maharaj, had taught them 300 years earlier. They were very careful not to take life. They did not kill animals for food. They only burned dead wood for fuel and they always checked it very carefully to make sure that there were no beetles or other small creatures crawling inside that would be burned in the fire. They tried to be calm and gentle with one another. And they took great care of their trees. But the ruler of the nearby lands was not so kind and gentle. He wanted wood for fuel and he had run out of wood on his own land because his men had cleared it. So he sent his soldiers to the land of the Bishnoi and told them to cut down all the trees there. The Bishnoi saw the soldiers approaching. They saw the axes in their hands, and they guessed what the soldiers were going to do. They ran to their trees and threw their arms around them to protect them. The ruler shouted at them to move. He warned them what would happen if they did not. But the Bishnoi would not move. They clung to their trees.

The ruler gave the order to move in, and the soldiers attacked, hacking away at the villagers so they could reach the trees. 363 of the Bishnoi died that day, before at last even the ruler was sickened by the sight and called his men off and went away leaving the Bishnoi in peace.

Not long afterwards, the Bishnoi built a temple to remember their ancestors who saved the trees and once a year they say special prayers for them.

In the time of the prophet Muhammad, there lived a boy who was usually very good but he had one great weakness, he was very fond of dates. He would stand at the bottom of the date trees and look up longingly, and his mouth would water at the thought of them. If only they would fall down quickly. One day he thought to himself, 'If I make the tree shake, then the dates will fall down and I will be able to eat them.'

So he took some large stones and pelted them at the long thin trunk of the tree, and sure enough the dates tumbled down and he was able to eat them.

Having discovered this trick, he threw stone after stone at the tree, shaking the branches but also pitting the trunk. He gave no thought to the damage he was causing the tree, but just enjoyed the dates which fell to his feet.

When the owners of the trees saw the damage that had been done, they were very angry and early the next day they lay in wait to catch the culprit. When the boy returned, the owners leapt out and seized him.

'Wait until the Prophet hears about this!' they shouted at him. 'He will be very angry!'

The boy shook with fear as he was hauled up before the Prophet and the owners proclaimed his crime. But the Prophet was not angry. He saw that the boy was not bad at heart. Instead he spoke to him gently and kindly, but very firmly.

'If you go on throwing stones at the trees,' he said, 'you will hurt the trees terribly. Then there will be no more dates, for the trees will not be able to grow them. Wait and eat the dates which have fallen on the ground.'

Then he blessed the boy and prayed that he would grow in wisdom.

Many ancient peoples knew that their lives were utterly dependent on the sun. Without it their crops wouldn't grow; without it there would be no day and night. They felt its warm gentle rays on their skin and saw the sun as loving, gentle and kind. Sometimes, however, it burned their skin and dried their crops and it was then that they also realised its awesome power.

And so it was that they worshipped the sun as the most powerful god, the giver of life. They sang its praises and they gave it gifts of sacrifices. The Aztecs in Central America even killed people to offer them up to the sun. They thought that the sun needed to be fed. The ancient Egyptians also worshipped the sun but they saw the sun as a loving god who gave life to all creation.

There is a song in the Bible which comes from Egypt. It was originally written as a song of praise to the sun by an Egyptian ruler, but one person who learned it thought to himself, 'This isn't about the sun. It is about our God who made the sun and the moon and the stars' and so he turned it into a song about God and it became part of the Bible.

Today we know that the earth, turning all the time, travels round the sun, rather than the sun travelling round the earth. However, as we have seen, people have not always known this. In the past they thought that the earth was at the centre of the universe. So why did people change their minds?

The first scientist to put forward the new theory was a mathematician and astronomer called Copernicus who lived 500 years ago. He studied the movement of the stars and the planets and worked out that the earth must go round the sun. But was he believed? Did people take his new theory seriously? With the exception of a few scientists, no they did not.

This was partly because they said, 'Look, we can see with our eyes that the sun moves round the earth.'

But there was another reason why people did not believe Copernicus. They did not want to believe him. When they thought that the earth was the centre of everything, they felt reassured that God cared about them, that the earth was important in God's sight. If the earth was only one of many planets going round the sun, then maybe it was not so important to God. That made them frightened. Even as much as 200 years later another astronomer, called Galileo, was punished for sharing Copernicus's views because his studies had confirmed them. But his work did, in the end, help to convince others that they had found the truth. Today there are very few who do not accept it.

The moon as a measure of time, page 84

Each night look up at the moon. What shape is it? Draw the shape of the moon each night in one of the circles.

Write the date of your first moon watch in this box ☐

Not only is the moon mysterious but because it changes over the month, it has often been used as a way of measuring the passing of time. 'When will you be back?' children would ask their fathers who were going off hunting in times gone by, and the fathers would reply, 'Before the full moon', or 'Before the new moon I will return.' The day was measured by the rising and setting of the sun but the weeks and months were measured by the moon.

The moon also told the people when to celebrate festivals. The new moon announces the start of festivals in the Jewish, Muslim and Christian faiths. Muslims have a whole month during which they eat and drink nothing from sunrise to sunset. They know the month of fasting has ended when the new moon appears in the night sky. Today it is possible to use calculations to predict accurately when the new moon will appear but many Muslims prefer not to know. If you say to them, 'When will your fast be over?' They reply, for example, 'Well, either Monday or Tuesday'. And when you say, 'But isn't it possible to use calculations to find out?' they say, 'Yes, it is. But we prefer that Allah tells us with the moon, rather than we tell Him.' So they look at the night sky and wait until the new moon indicates it is time for the festival.

Today modern people living in cities are often very good at reading clocks and calendars. They are not so good at reading nature. They aren't as good at guessing the time of day from the sun, and they rarely notice the shape of the moon. They have learned how to read clocks but they have forgotten how to read the sky. In forgetting this, have we lost something important?

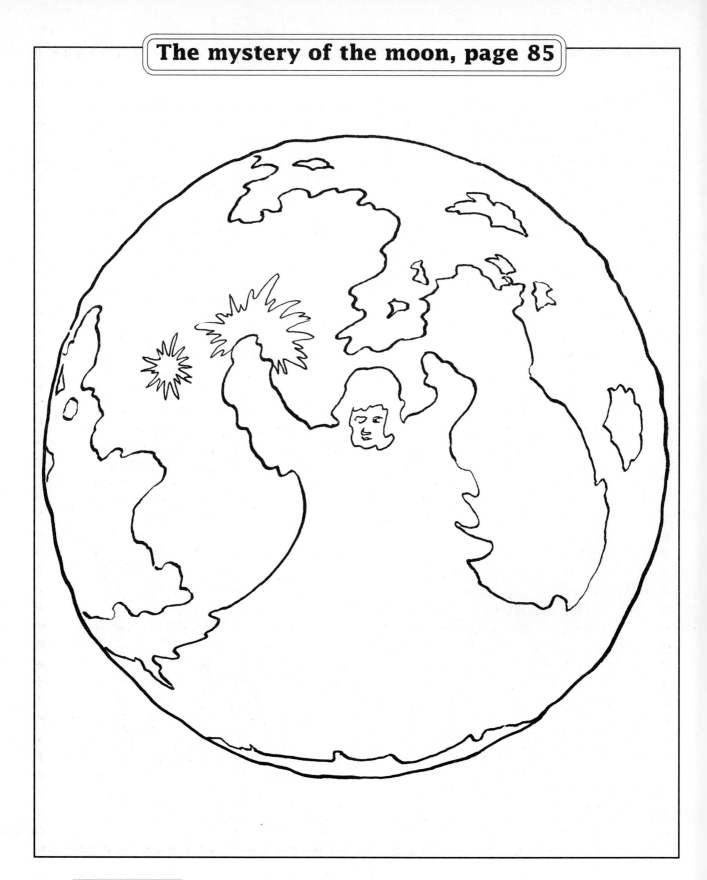

Once, long, long ago, a wicked king lived in China. His people lived in terror of him for he only knew how to do evil. They longed for the day that he would die, and they would be free of him.

But the king was determined not to die. He wanted to go on living for ever and ever. So when he heard that somewhere, far across the sea, there was a magic potion which could enable a person to live forever, his cruel heart leapt with joy and he determined that he would possess that potion. So he sent out his ships to the furthest corners of the earth to find it.

After many adventures the crew of one of the ships found the magic potion and brought it home. When the king saw it he rubbed his hands in glee and set the bottle on a shelf where he could see it and gloat over it. In the morning he would summon his cowering court to him and drink in triumph before them.

Throughout the land the people sorrowed at the thought that such a wicked king could live forever.

Now although the king was bad, he had a kind and loving wife whose name was Sheung Ngao. It grieved her to see the people suffer and when she learned that the potion of everlasting life had been found, she knew that no matter what she must prevent her husband from drinking it. Her own safety didn't count, whatever the king did to her did not matter.

That night in the dark, she crept stealthily into his room to steal away the potion. But her husband stirred in his sleep and saw her. He sprang forth to kill her and rescue the potion. But Sheung Ngao poured it down her own throat. The king roared with anger and was about to grab her when the gods lifted her out of his grasp and carried her to the moon.

Did the potion of everlasting life work? Yes it did, for Sheung Ngao lives on the moon to this day.

Every year now the Chinese people remember the story of the bravery of Sheung Ngao at the Moon Festival, when the full moon seems bigger and brighter than at any other point in the year. For days beforehand they make paper lanterns in the shapes of fish, birds and other animals, and then the people process through the streets, celebrating the beauty of the moon and the blessings she sends on the earth.

Over the centuries men, women and children have looked up at the moon and wondered at its silvery beauty. Some have longed to hold it in their hands. The Ancient Greeks thought there was a goddess of the moon who protected all young women and women in childbirth.
(*Here have the child dressed as the moon goddess move across the centre stage.*)

Many Chinese people throughout the world celebrate the beauty and the mystery of the moon with a moon festival in the Autumn. They have street processions with lanterns.
(*Switch the lights off and have a lantern procession round the hall, with some children carrying the paper lanterns, others carrying the torches.*)

Things have changed because of scientific discoveries. The moon is no longer so mysterious and men have walked on it.
(*Ask the children to act out the first lunar landing.*)

Here we have seen two different views of the moon; the beautiful and mysterious heavenly body that we see from earth, and the dry and dusty surface that men have walked on. Is one of these views right and the other wrong? Is the moon any less beautiful or mysterious because men have walked on her surface?

Masks, page 88

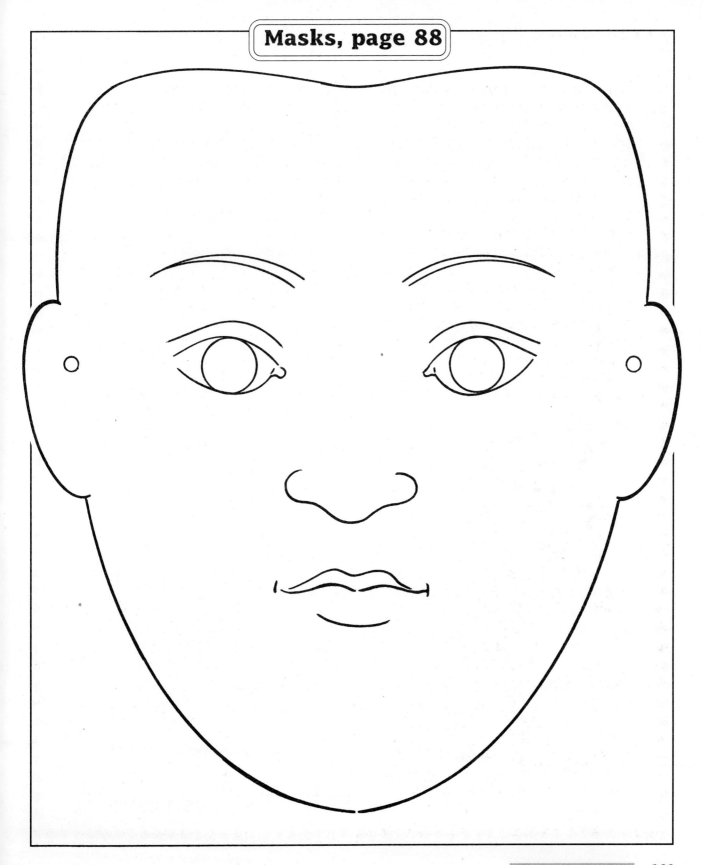

It seemed like an answer to prayer. For thousands of years, people had wanted to find a way of getting rid of flies, mosquitoes, fleas and other such pests. Farmers lost a lot of their crops to such pests. Doctors wanted to get rid of disease-carrying pests like mosquitoes.

Then it was discovered that a powerful chemical combination could destroy such insects and pests. It is known as DDT. Its real name is Dichlorodiphenyltrichloroethane. You can see why it is usually called DDT.

It was put to work straight away. Soldiers fighting in the Second World War discovered that it got rid of the lice that crawled all over their bodies, causing irritation and making them want to scratch. Farmers found it wiped out insects which attacked their crops and made them unfit for human consumption. The way DDT killed off mosquitoes gave many people hope that soon mosquitoes would die out and the terrible disease of malaria would be gone forever. It seemed like a wonderful invention. It looked as if it only did good and, at first, this was the case. Fewer people fell ill from diseases carried by insects. More food was produced because pests had not destroyed the crops. All seemed fine but it was not.

As early as the 1950's bird-watchers and others working in the countryside began to notice that there were fewer birds around, particularly birds of prey such as falcons and kestrels. As they investigated, it began to look as though DDT was killing not just the pests but also birds and other forms of wildlife. However the big companies who made DDT were not convinced. They didn't want to be convinced. They were making lots of money from selling it and they wanted to go on selling it.

Gradually, more and more evidence was found to show that DDT was damaging the whole of the world's wildlife. It was certainly killing pests, but once it had been sprayed on plants, it soaked into the ground. From there it went into the streams and rivers. Scientists found that it was killing thousands of creatures. It was making the shells of birds' eggs so thin that many eggs were breaking and being lost before the mother birds could hatch them. It was discovered that even the Antarctic, which is hundreds of miles away from anywhere where DDT was sprayed, had got DDT in its snow and ice and in the bodies of animals like polar bears.

By the late 1960's, it was obvious that there was a danger of DDT poisoning the whole planet. DDT was found in the bodies of young children because almost all food now had DDT in it. Wild birds were dying out all across Europe where much of the DDT had been sprayed. Gradually the big companies realised that they would have to stop using DDT. It had certainly helped save many lives at first. But now it was a terrible threat to the well-being of many birds, animals and even human beings. However, because it was so useful, many people wanted to go on using it.

'You do not have absolute proof that it is doing any harm,' they said. 'We must have proof before we stop using it.'

But slowly the protesters won by showing clear evidence that DDT was poisoning the world. In 1984 the British Government finally banned the use of DDT in Britain.

DDT was a great invention. It was used because people wanted to help make the world a better place, but it ended up doing more damage than it did good.

CAUTION
DDT SPRAYING
IN PROGRESS

All went well as the men travelled across the plain to the town. On the way back to the village, one man said, 'Wait a minute, don't you think we had better stop and see that we are all here, safe and sound?' So they all stopped and he counted, 'One, two, three, four, five, six, seven, eight, nine. Nine! Nine! But there were ten men who set out!'

'You must have made a mistake,' said another. 'Let me count. One, two, three, four, five, six, seven, eight, nine.'

They all counted and they all got the same answer of 'nine'. Ten men had set out and now one was missing! That could only mean one thing. He had been snatched by a leopard as they had walked in single file across the plain.

They sat down by the path and wailed, 'Our brother has been taken by a leopard! Even now the fearsome creature is gnawing at his skin. Oh, his poor wife! Oh, his poor children!'

They could not tell who had been killed. They only knew that ten men had set out and now they had counted only nine men returning.

Sorrowfully, the men picked up their sacks of flour and walked on, weeping as they went.

When they arrived at the village, the people crowded round to hear what had happened. 'Our brother was killed by a leopard!' they cried, and someone started to beat the funeral drum.

But one small girl was puzzled. She saw the bags of flour and she counted them. 'One, two, three, four, five, six, seven, eight, nine, ten.' There were ten bags of flour. If there are ten bags of flour there must have been ten men.

She tugged at her mother's skirts. 'There are ten bags of flour,' she said. 'There must be ten men.'

Her mother looked and counted. 'Why, yes, there are ten men!' she exclaimed.

'What?' cried the men. 'Ten men! Why our brother must have escaped. He must have struggled with that fearsome leopard and run to join us. How brave he is!'

And from that day to this, the story is told of the brave villager who was seized by a leopard but managed to kill it and return home safely.

The game of chess was invented many centuries ago in China. An old story says that the inventor was a man who was very, very clever – a mathematical genius. He must have been because chess is a game which challenges some of the cleverest people in the world.

The story also says that the Emperor of China was so pleased with the game that he said that the inventor could choose his own reward.

'Your royal graciousness,' replied the inventor, bowing low to the ground, 'I would like the following. Please put a grain of rice on the first square of the chessboard, and then double the number on the next square. Double it again on the next, and the next until the last square.'

'I have got away lightly,' thought the emperor. 'For what is a few sacks of rice to a powerful man like me?'

Out loud he said, 'That seems a fitting reward for the inventor of the chessboard.' And he ordered his servants to fetch a bag of rice. They began to count out the grains of rice. (*Count out the rice with the children until it becomes clear just how much rice is involved.*)

By the time they had reached the sixteenth square, the emperor was beginning to see his foolish mistake. Bag after bag of rice was fetched but it was still not enough. By the time they had reached the thirty-second square he knew that there would not be enough rice in the whole of the land to fulfil his promise. The inventor of chess was a mathematical genius. The emperor had proved himself a mathematical fool.

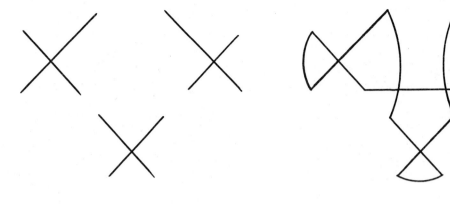

*Worksheet reproduced by kind permission of F. Russell
Clampitt of Heald Place Primary School, Manchester.*

These patterns are often found in mosques, the Muslim place of communal prayer. Sometimes they are woven into the carpet but in many parts of the world they are painted on to tiles. Some of the patterns are over a thousand years old. One of the reasons why Muslims use these patterns is that they want to show that life should be governed by God's rules, just like the pattern is determined by set rules.

Muslims believe that God shows his people His rules in the Qur'an and that everything in life must be consistent with the same rules. Some other faiths, too, believe that God has made rules for the world.

Muslims believe that if we all followed the rules properly, then life would be beautiful just as these patterns are beautiful.

Elizabeth and her dad were busy preparing a barbecue in the garden when a small dog appeared, it seemed, out of nowhere.

'It must be that dog which is visiting next door,' said Dad and he picked up the dog and dropped it over the fence.

A short time later there was a scrabbling sound. The dog was squirming its way back through the fence. Dad tried to block the hole but he couldn't. He would fill the hole but no sooner had he turned his back then the dog appeared again. It must have smelled the meat.

'It's no good,' sighed Dad. 'We'll have to drop a note in next door and tell them we've got the dog in here.'

Elizabeth was delighted. She loved dogs and she spent the afternoon playing with it. They had to give up on the barbecue though, as the dog kept pinching the sausages.

When the people from next door got back though, they said it wasn't the dog that was visiting them after all, and no they didn't know who it belonged to.

'Please, Dad. Can we keep it, Dad? Please, please, please,' Elizabeth pleaded.

'No,' said Dad 'we can't. It's only a little mongrel, but I should think there's probably someone who loves it. A little girl like you, perhaps, and she would miss it if it didn't return. Let's look and see if it has a number on its collar.'

Sure enough there was a phone number. They rang it, but there was no reply. They kept on ringing all that evening; still no reply.

'I hope they never reply,' thought Elizabeth. 'I hope I can keep it and if I do I'll call it 'Surprise' because it surprised me. It might look a bit odd; only a mongrel, isn't that what Dad said? But I think it's lovely.'

There was a reply, though, the next morning. And the voice on the end of the phone sounded very relieved at the news that the little dog was safe and well.

'What mix of breeds is it?' asked Dad when the owner came to pick the dog up. 'It is a mongrel, isn't it?'

'A mongrel!' laughed the owner. 'A mongrel! That's a rare breed, that one. It's worth three hundred pounds!'

'Three hundred pounds!' they couldn't believe it. 'Three hundred pounds!'

Elizabeth had a good cry when the dog left. She had grown to love it, and she knew her dad would never spend three hundred pounds to buy a dog, especially when dogs cost a lot to feed as well.

However, not long afterwards, Elizabeth and her dad went down to the Dogs' Home and chose a small, lost dog who had no home. It didn't cost them three hundred pounds to buy it. In fact it didn't cost them anything at all, but Elizabeth loved her new little dog just as much. She could not have loved it more if it had been worth a million pounds! And she called this dog 'Surprise'.

Once in India there was a rich and successful merchant called Duni Chand. He had worked all his life and now he lived in great luxury. He was proud of his wealth and liked to show off about it. Every year he held a big banquet to which he invited all the local religious leaders. He hoped that if he pleased them his spirit and the spirits of his family would be better off when they died.

The wise Guru Nanak was passing near the city one year at the time of the feast. When Duni Chand heard he was close by, he sent Guru Nanak an invitation to the feast which Guru Nanak was glad to accept.

The wise man, Guru Nanak, and the rich man, Duni Chand, sat side by side at the feast.

'This is a most wonderful meal,' said the Guru. 'But tell me, I am new to this city and there is one thing I do not understand. Why is it that there are seven flags on your front door. What do they mean?'

'Why that is easy to answer,' replied the rich man. 'It is a local custom to show how wealthy you are. Each flag represents a thousand silver coins. Everyone who passes by my house looks at my door and sees seven flags and knows that I have stored seven thousand silver coins, and they can see what a very wealthy man I am, and how important I am.'

'Oh,' said Guru Nanak, and he paused for a moment. Duni Chand thought that the Guru looked very impressed. Then the Guru bent down and took from his bag a needle he had been using to sew up sacks. He gave the needle to Duni Chand, saying, 'Please will you keep this needle safe for me and give it to me in the next life.'

Duni Chand looked at the needle. He was very puzzled. How could he return the needle to the Guru in the next life? He couldn't take the needle with him when he died. Then he realised if he couldn't take a needle, then he couldn't take seven thousand silver coins with him either.

He turned again to the Guru. 'I see I have been foolish,' he said. 'What shall I do now?'

'Share your wealth with others,' answered the Guru, 'that's what's important in life, not storing it up in bags.'

And that is what Duni Chand did. He shared his wealth with the poor in the community.

Guru Nanak encouraged the rich to share their wealth with others. Jesus did the same. Once he told a rich young ruler to sell all he had and to give the money to the poor.

Have you ever longed for something so much that you would give everything you had for it?

Isaac had twin sons, Jacob and Esau. They were brothers, born on the same day but they were very different men. Jacob had smooth skin but Esau's was rough and hairy. Jacob was a farmer who grew crops. His life was spent tilling the fields, sowing seeds and harvesting grain. Often he cooked up the grain into delicious soups. Esau was a hunter. His days were spent chasing animals for meat.

The brothers were not friends. In fact, they had never been friends. They had come out of their mother's womb fighting and they had been fighting ever since.

Esau was the eldest, the first-born, but only by a matter of minutes. But because he was the first-born, according to the rule of those times in that place, he would inherit the birthright and would be the next leader of the community. Oh, how Jacob envied that birthright! Oh, how he longed for it! He wanted it more than anything in the world. He would give anything for it.

One evening Jacob sat stoking the fire. He had  made a pot of vegetable stew. It simmered and steamed. It smelt delicious. In staggered Esau, tired and very, very, hungry after a long day of hunting.

'Oh! What a wonderful smell!' he sighed as he flung his hunting equipment down. 'I would give anything for a bowl of that stew. I'm starving.'

Jacob's eyes lit up. 'Anything?' he asked.

'Yes, anything,' replied his brother as the pangs of hunger gnawed away at his stomach.

'Would you give away your birthright?' Jacob said tentatively. 'Would you sell me your birthright for a bowl of my stew?'

Esau was so hungry he didn't even stop to think what he was saying. 'Yes', he said. 'Give me a pot of soup and I'll give you my birthright.'

And so it was that Esau sold the right to be leader of the community, his birthright, to his brother Jacob.

Jacob had to trick his father to claim that birthright but that's another story.

Jacob did become the leader of the Hebrew people but gaining that cost him dearly. He lost his father's love and he had to go into exile for many long years.

Bibliography

Introduction
Alternative Service Book (1980) Hodder/SPCK
Education Reform Act (1988) HMSO
Handbook for Agreed Syllabus Conferences, SACREs and Schools (1989) Religious Education Council
Marshall-Taylor, Geoffrey (1990) *The Complete Come and Praise*, BBC Books

Chapter 1
Ahlberg, Allan (1984) *Please, Mrs Butler*, Puffin Books
Wild Goose Worship Group (1989) *A Wee Worship Book*, Wild Goose Publications, The Iona Community, 840 Govan Road, Glasgow G51 3UU

Chapter 2
Hymns Ancient and Modern, New Standard Version (1983) Hymns Ancient and Modern Ltd
Ahlberg, Allan and Janet (1983) *Peepo!* Penguin
Foster, John (1965) *They Converted Our Ancestors*, SCM Press
Hughes, Shirley (1979) *Dogger*, Picture Lions
Marshall, Sherrin (Ed.) (1989) *Women in Reformation and Counter-Reformation Europe*, Indiana University Press
Roberts, Frank (1992) *India 1526-1800*, Hodder & Stoughton
Waddell, Martin (1989) *Grandma's Bill*, Simon and Schuster
Wigner, Annabel (1987) *Elizabeth and Akbar: Portraits of Power*, Stanley Thorne

Chapter 3
Breuilly, Elizabeth and Palmer, Sandra (1992) *REAL Scheme: A Tapestry of Tales* Collins Educational
Gadsby, David and Hoggarth, John (1980) *Alleluya! 77 songs for thinking people*, A & C Black
Hilton, Donald (Ed.) (1991) *Liturgy of Life*, NCEC
Hughes, Shirley (1976) *Sally's Secret*, Penguin
Hutchins, Pat (1978) *The Wind Blew*, Penguin
Sarwar, Ghulam (1984) *The Children's Book of Salah*, The Muslim Educational Trust

Chapter 4
Assisi Declarations (1986) WWF
Coventry Cathedral Creation Festival Liturgy (1988) WWF
Anno, Mitsumasa (1985) *Anno's Counting Book*, Macmillan's Children's Books
Breuilly, Elizabeth and Palmer, Sandra (1992) *REAL Scheme: Infant*

Assembly Book, Collins Educational
Dahl, Tessa (1988) *The Same But Different*, Hamish Hamilton
Eliot, TS (1940) *Old Possum's Book of Practical Cats*, Faber
Herriot, James (1986) *The Christmas Day Kitten*, M Joseph
Hutchins, Pat (1974) *Titch*, Penguin
Milne, AA (1965) *Now We Are Six*, Methuen
Pinto, Vivian De Sola and Roberts, F. Warren (Eds) (1981) *The Complete Poems of DH Lawrence*, Penguin
Rose, Deborah Lee (1990) *The People Who Hugged Trees*, Robert Rhinehart (US)
Simmonds, Posy (1987) *Fred*, Cape
Spier, Peter (1981) *People*, World's Work
Sutton, Eve and Dodd, Lynley (1978) *My Cat Likes to Hide in Boxes*, Penguin
Travers, PL (1982) *Mary Poppins*, Collins
Webb, Kaye (Ed.) (1979) *I Like This Poem: Favourite poems chosen by children*, Penguin

Chapter 5
Carroll, Lewis (1984) *Alice in Wonderland*, Penguin
Reith, Martin (1975) *God in Our Midst*, SPCK

Chapter 6
Blake, Howard (1986) *The Snowman: Easy Piano Picture Book*, Faber
Briggs, Raymond (1978) *The Snowman*, Hamish Hamilton
Dahl, Roald (1982) *George's Marvellous Medicine*, Penguin
Gray, Nigel (1990) *A Balloon for Grandad*, Picture Lions
Hughes, Shirley (1985) *Lucy and Tom's Christmas*, Picture Lions
Pirotta, Saviour (1990) *Do You Believe in Magic?* Dent Children's Books
Robinson, Joan G. (1975) *About Teddy Robinson*, Penguin
Wells, Rosemary (1978) *Noisy Nora*, Picture Lions
Wells, Rosemary (1983) *Timothy Goes to School*, Picture Lions

Additional picture books
Craft, Ruth and Haas, Irene (1980) *Carrie Hepple's Garden*, Collins
Havill, Juanita (1990) *Jamaica's Find*, Little Mammoth
Hughes, Shirley (1985) *Alfie Gives a Hand*, Picture Lions
Keller, Holly (1990) *Goodbye Max*, Walker Books
Sendak, Maurice (1973) *In the Night Kitchen*, Penguin
Sendak, Maurice (1973) *Where the Wild Things Are*, Penguin
Varley, Susan (1985) *Badger's Parting*

Gifts, Picture Lions
Walsh, Jill Paton (1985) *Babylon*, Beaver Books

Chapter 7
Books on festivals
The Way We Live series, Evans, includes titles on particular festivals.
Brown, Alan (Ed.) on behalf of Shap Working Party on World Religions in Education (1986) *Festivals in World Religions*, Longman
Bennett, Olivia (1984) *Exploring Religion: Festivals*, Harper Collins
Bennett, Olivia (1986) *Festival!* series, Thomas Nelson
Palmer, Martin (1984) *Faiths and Festivals*, Ward Lock Educational
Priestly, Jack (Series Ed.) *Living Festivals series* (22 books), Chanceter

Useful addresses

Resources
Down Under Map of the World available from Universal Press Pty. Ltd., 64 Talavera Road, North Ryde, New South Wales 2113, Australia
Yanomamo by Peter Rose and Anne Conlon (WWF/Joseph Weinberger) available from WWF (see below)

Environmental concern
Greenpeace, Canonbury Villas, Islington, London N1 2PN
Information (only) on WWF resources from Publishing Unit (Education), WWF UK, Panda House, Weyside Park, Cattleshall Lane, Godalming, Surrey GU7 1XR

International aid organisations
Anti-slavery International, 180 Brixton Road, London SW9 6AT
Barnardos, Tanner Lane, Barkingside, Ilford, Essex IG6 1QG
Christian Aid, Education Sector, 35 Lower Marsh, London SE1 7RL
Oxfam, Education Section, 274 Banbury Road, Oxford OX2 7DZ
Save the Children Fund, Central Information Office, 17 Grove Lane, Camberwell, London SE5 8RD
Tear Fund (Resources), 100 Church Road, Teddington, Middlesex TW11 8QE

Coventry Cathedral peace ministries
Community of the Cross of Nails, Canon Heather Wallis (Peace and Reconciliation Ministry) and/or Peace Ministry, Canon Paul Oestricher, Director of International Ministry both at Cathedral Offices, 7 Priory Row, Coventry, West Midlands CV1 5ES